THE
Satires
OF
Horace

THE
Satires
OF
Horace

Translated by

A. M. Juster

Introduction by

Susanna Braund

PENN

UNIVERSITY OF PENNSYLVANIA PRESS
PHILADELPHIA

Published by
University of Pennsylvania Press
Philadelphia, Pennsylvania 19104-4112

Printed in the United States of America on acid-free paper
10 9 8 7 6 5 4 3 2 1

Library of Congress Cataloging-in-Publication Data
Horace.
[Satirae. English]
The satires of Horace / translated by A. M. Juster ; introduction by Susanna Braund.
     p.   c.m.
Includes bibliographical references and index.
ISBN 978-0-8122-4090-0 (alk. paper)
   1. Verse satire, Latin—Translations into English. 2. Rome—Poetry.
I. Juster, A. M., 1956– II. Title.
PA6396.S3J87 2008
871′.01—dc22   2008010527

"Into what fictive realms can imagination
Translate you, Flaccus, and your kin?"

—W. H. AUDEN

Contents

Translator's Note

Wrestling with Horace's *Satires* word by word and line by line was a privilege, but also an enormous frustration. All translators who take on important poetry fail; the only questions are "By how much?" and "In what ways?"

I translated the *Satires* because I believed that the other available translations failed to capture the essence of the work—its wit and tone—in a way I thought should be attempted. I started from the simple premise that readers deserved a faithful version of the *Satires* that was fun to read.

Hundreds of poets from Milton to Pound have translated Horace's odes. However, few contemporary poets have taken on the *Satires*—undoubtedly because we lack free verse models for extended satirical poetry.

Until the twentieth century, translations of the *Satires* and similar works relied on traditional forms, meters, and assumptions of the English light verse tradition. Generally these efforts were peppy and popular, if often so cavalier about the meaning of the texts that they were desecrations. The last major formal translation of the *Satires* was John Conington's in 1874. As with Pope's imitations of the *Satires*, Conington used heroic couplets; despite its deficiencies Conington's take on the *Satires* was the standard for many years.

In the twentieth century, translation of the *Satires* became the province of academics who largely drained the text of its vigor, wit, and conversational tone. The 1926 Fairclough version (Harvard University Press) is reasonably accurate but prose. The 1959 Bovie version (University of Chicago Press) is a "sixties" precursor loaded with trendy extratextual references ranging from *Paradise Lost* to existentialism. The 1973 Rudd version (Penguin) claims to be written in hexameter, but it is in fact a prose translation that tangles sense and syntax by forcing Horace's many long sentences into an order dictated by line-by-line translation rather than fluidity.

The 1993 "literal" translations of Brown and Muecke (Aris & Phillips) are extremely well done and their notes were invaluable to me. Their work, however, has the weakness of all such translations—it is tough reading because it is meant for scholars parsing the Latin and not for general readers who can't access the Latin.

The most recent literary translation, the 1996 Alexander version (Princeton University Press), rests on a seriously mistaken premise. Alexander declares about the *Satires* that "Though written in hexameters they are *prose through and through*" (emphasis added). He compounds this error by adding that with regard to meter "all of this I have dispensed with and listened instead to Horace's pulsations; and having ascertained the rhythmic pattern, I have not sought to reproduce (which is impossible in the crossover of languages) but to recreate an English equivalent which should be true to the genius of our language and yet be related (at least as blood cousins are related) to the Latin original."

Despite the grandiosity of Alexander's description of his own work, it is impossible to discern any rhythmic patterns in his translation; the truth is that it is generic contemporary free verse that lacks any connection to form, much less to Horatian meters and rhythms. His version is also frequently off-key, primarily due to his misconception of Horace as "the quintessential Italian" rather than the quintessential Roman.

I confess fondness for William Matthews's unfinished 2002 version (Ausable Press). It captures much of the fluidity and concision of the Satires, although these virtues frequently come at the price of eliminating content essential to understanding the subtlety of the text. If Matthews had lived long enough to complete and revise this work, it might well have become the standard.

So, how *should* the *Satires* be translated? Except perhaps for Billy Collins and a few others, wit is rare in today's free verse, and nobody has written an acclaimed long humorous poem in free verse. Whether it is fashionable in the academy or not, the ghosts of Swift and Pope still haunt our expectations of satire and humor. The trick is not how to run from that legacy, but how to respect it with fresh language that does not savage the original poem.

My first rule for this translation was to preserve as many meanings and images from the original text as possible. My second rule was to inject nothing into the translation that isn't arguably in the original. When jokes just didn't translate well, I bent these rules a little and confessed the liberty in the notes.

A corollary of my first rule was to use names of people and places without dumbing them down, a surprisingly common practice. Rudd, for instance, calls Porcius "Hogg," Novius "Newman," and, most annoyingly, Horace "Floppy" when Horace refers to himself as "Flaccus." I considered my corollary sufficiently important that I necessarily deviated slightly from my strict meter and rhyme so I could include names that flavor the poetry and that might stimulate readers to learn more about the context of the Satires.

I wrote this translation not just in meter, but in rhymed iambic pentameter couplets, otherwise known as "heroic couplets." I am well aware that this choice will be controversial among classicists. Rudd, for instance, has asserted that "the obvious fact remains that rhyming couplets would not do for a modern translation. They do not allow the thought to flow on in a conversational style, and they demand conventional licenses of diction and word-order which are not granted today."

Rudd's argument is, of course, impossible to defend. Horace himself argued in metrical verse for the importance of meter, and there is nothing about formal poetry that requires mangling diction and word order. I challenge anyone to scour the couplets in Richard Wilbur's Molière translations for "conventional licenses of diction and word order which are not granted today," then to contrast the clarity and beauty of Wilbur's lines with Rudd's rendering of lines 36–40 of Book I, Satire 2:

> It is worth your while to give ear, ye who wish ill success
> to adulterous men, how on all sides they are beset by troubles,
> how their pleasure is spoiled by many a pain, is won but rarely,
> and then, as it often chances, amidst atrocious perils.

Enough said on that point.

Roman meters relied on syllable length rather than stress, so Horace's dactylic hexameter doesn't feel much like English dactylic hexameter. Indeed, today's formal poets rarely use dactylic hexameter because the line length and rhythms tend to sound alien to our ear. It was, however, the workhorse meter of Horace's age, and thus is arguably closest in spirit to our iambic pentameter.

I have chosen to use rhyme, even though the Romans did not, because it is so embedded in our expectations of humorous poetry. The combination of rhyme and meter creates rhythms that lead to the expectation of a punch line, and the anticipation of the punch line is a key element of humor. Most of my rhymes are exact if one relies on my idiosyncratic American pronunciation (apologies to my British friends for "filleted"). I bent a bit to preserve a few names, and I used identical rhyme, otherwise known as "rime riche," on the two occasions where Horace repeated a closing word or phrase from the previous line.

I have used fewer metrical substitutions than Horace did, but I have used some. I have made frequent use of the convention of starting a line with a trochee rather than an iamb, and I have also used trochees to start sentences later in a line. As is common practice, I have also occasionally used substituted trochees to signal a shift to a darker mood.

I have generally avoided anapestic substitutions except to preserve a name, and have used elision only when it is standard in everyday speech. I have also tried to track everyday pronunciation in my scansion, thus I counted "fire" as a two-syllable word that rhymes with "higher," even though most formal poets of today still follow older conventions with regard to many words of this type.

I hear more spondees (a foot of two syllables of approximately equal stress) than most formalists, and I have made many of what I consider to be spondaic substitutions. I also adamantly reject the notion that all stressed syllables must be hard stresses, and encourage those interested in prosody to embrace Timothy Steele's analysis of "relative stress" in his *all the fun's in how you say a thing* (Ohio University Press, 1999).

When I ended a line with a feminine ending (an extra unstressed syllable at the end of the line), I gave myself the option of making the next line either a "headless" (first unstressed syllable dropped) or a standard iambic pentameter line. Practice varies, and I usually used the headless lines to make enjambed lines flow without a break in the rhythm. I have also avoided capitalizing the first word in each line because I thought to do so would distract the reader in the enjambed lines that attempt to mimic Horace's enjambment.

I tried to replicate puns when I could, and used wordplay in the vicinity of puns when I could not pun more precisely. I also tried to avoid words and tropes with too much of a modern connotation (I reluctantly gave up on "waffling" at one point for this reason), but occasionally allowed myself some liberties.

For all the years of frustration, this project gave me great joy. I hope it gives you great joy as well.

Introduction

SUSANNA BRAUND

For us in the twenty-first century, "satire" denotes a form of wittily savage social and political discourse that pillories public figures, often with no-holds-barred abandon. But how does our concept of satire relate to Roman satire, a literary form that the Romans claim to have invented themselves? Only obliquely. There is no doubt that the idea of satire as a crafted form of abuse derives from authors of Roman satire, above all Juvenal, who was writing more than a century after Horace and who gave us the phrase "bread and circuses" (*panem et circenses*). But not all Roman satirists were as fierce or direct as Juvenal. Horace seems so mild by comparison with his later fellow-satirist that it may seem hard to believe they are both deploying the same genre. What they share, in contradistinction from modern satirists, is their use of a specialized poetic form. Roman verse satire is written in the dactylic hexameter meter, a highly stylized form borrowed from epic poetry. The Roman satirists often seem aware of the huge gap between their often disgusting and mundane material and the heroic achievements recorded in the same meter by the likes of Homer and Virgil. A. M. Juster's bold and brilliant choice of rhymed iambic pentameter couplets (also known as heroic couplets) for this new translation of Horace's *Satires* acknowledges the significance of poetic form in a way impossible for translations in prose or in free verse. When we read this translation, if we find ourselves thinking of more elevated poetry in the same meter—for example, Dryden's translation of Virgil's *Aeneid* or Pope's translation of the *Iliad*—this means that the translator has succeeded at duplicating the effect that Horace's hexameters must have had on his contemporary audience.

So, although we might think we know what to expect from "satire," it is important to remember that Horace's *Satires* in the genre of *satura* are the product of a society that is alien as well as familiar. A sketch of Horace's social, political, and literary contexts will enhance understanding of what he was doing in these poems. Let us start with his life and times.

Horace—Quintus Horatius Flaccus, to give him his full Roman name—lived during momentous times that saw the transition from Republic to Principate. Born in 65 B.C.E., for much of his life he moved in elite circles at Rome, even though his background was relatively lowly. He was the son of a freedman—a former slave—who had made a fortune from entrepreneurship and who bought the best possible education for his son. That meant taking him to Rome from Apulia, in the far south of Italy. Horace completed his education alongside sons of the elite with a long stay in Athens. There, in 44 B.C.E., he joined the retinue of Brutus (the assassin of Julius Caesar), who promoted him to a position carrying equestrian status—the second highest rank at Rome, exceeded only by senatorial rank. But his promising career was soon checked by Brutus' rout and suicide at the battle of Philippi in 42, which had a negative impact on Horace's economic as well as social and political status. Shrewdly, he took the post of permanent assistant to the quaestors' office (*scriba quaestorii*), which handled public finances and public records. This position provided him with considerable influence and income. His friendship with the poet Virgil, future author of the *Aeneid*, facilitated an introduction first to the powerful patron Maecenas in 38 and then to Maecenas' friend Octavian, the future emperor Augustus. From that point onward, Horace's position was secure—so secure that he later felt able to decline Augustus' invitation to become his private secretary. At his death he named the emperor as heir and was buried near his patron Maecenas.

Horace's poetic output is prolific and spans a range of literary genres. His first venture was a first book of *Satires*, written in hexameters and published in 35–34 B.C.E. The second book of *Satires*, along with a book of fierce iambic poems called *Epodes*, followed soon after the crucial battle of Actium (31) that established Octavian in sole power. But Horace is best known for his lyric poetry, known collectively as *Odes*, in which he explores a wide range of political, moral, amatory, and poetic themes. In *Odes* 1–3, published as a collection in 23 B.C.E, Horace repeatedly demonstrates his allegiance to Augustus' new regime. Augustus returned the compliment by commissioning from him the *carmen saeculare*—"Hymn for the Era"—for performance at his celebration of the Secular Games in 17 B.C.E. The rest of Horace's poetic output is harder to date. At some point, he returned to the hexameter for *Epistles* Books I and II and for the so-called *Ars Poetica* (which is really an extension of his verse *Epistles*); his final engagement with lyric produced *Odes* 4, dating from 13 B.C.E. Despite some pressure and expectation, he never undertook an epic poem in praise of Augustus and defends himself (rather feebly) for this decision in both his *Satires* and his *Odes.* But both he and Augustus were well aware that Horace had celebrated many aspects of the Augustan program in other genres of poetry.

In his early poetic career, Horace experimented with two literary forms of attack—the old tradition of savage iambic poetry, long established in Greek literature, and the relatively recent Roman invention of hexametric satiric poetry. It is telling that he abandoned iambic poetry after just one book (*Epodes*), while he returned to the hexameter not only for a second book of *Satires* but also for all his *Epistles*, which share so many features with the *Satires* that many scholars follow Horace's hint (*Epistles* II.2.59–60) and regard them as belonging to the same genre. What appealed to him about the Roman genre and how does he relate to earlier satire? These questions are worth asking because the Greco-Roman world gave greater attention than our contemporary world does to the tradition within which an artist or poet worked and tended to measure a poet's achievements in terms of his relationship to his predecessors.

The genre of verse satire had received definitive shape about a hundred years before Horace took it up from a member of the Roman aristocracy called Gaius Lucilius (perhaps 180–102 B.C.E.). Unfortunately, only fragments of his poems survive—but enough to show the huge influence he had on Horace. It is no surprise that Horace calls him the "inventor" of the genre. After experimenting with many different meters, Lucilius settled on the hexameter as the meter for his satires. This decision to hijack the meter of epic—the most elevated literary genre in the Greco-Roman world, a form devoted to celebrating the exploits of heroes, kings and generals—must have created an astonishing conflict between form and content for the Roman audience. In his *Satires*, Lucilius attacked both eminent and lowly individuals for a wide range of personal failings ranging from incompetence to arrogance. He satirized city life with its frantic competitiveness and self-indulgent luxury. He criticized superstition and parodied philosophical ideas. And all this he did in the first person. Lucilius' autobiographical stance (whether or not it reflects anything at all about the real Lucilius) is a lasting legacy to the genre. So too is his unelevated style of diction: conversational, rambling, even blunt and obscene. He sometimes incorporates Greek words into his Latin and invents neologisms for effect; he sometimes indulges in epic parody. How did Horace develop the genre from the vigor and directness of the "inventor" of Roman satire?

Horace is certainly explicit about his admiration for Lucilius. Several times in the *Satires* (I.4, I.10, II.1) he evaluates Lucilius' poetry, and he also pays him the compliment of imitating him in several poems. For example, his account of his journey to Brundisium (modern Brindisi), Satire I.5, is clearly inspired by a Lucilius poem describing a journey to Sicily; for the ancients, imitation was a form of homage. In Horace's eyes, Lucilius was a fearless and witty critic of socially unacceptable behavior, but he was also prolix, writing too much too fast. Horace excuses his predecessor as a product of his times: "if fate could put him here today, / he would revise far more and hack away / at excess verbiage." It seems clear that Horace regards himself as the natural urbane and suave successor to the "inventor" of the genre.

One manifestation of Horace's self-conscious urbanity is the high degree of self-irony that informs his autobiographical presentation. The self-ironic persona was something pioneered by Lucilius, but in Horace's hands it reaches new heights. For example, Horace takes a position of extreme humility by self-deprecatingly calling himself "a freedman's son" repeatedly in Satire I.6. In Satire I.5 he describes a wet dream after being disappointed by a girlfriend, and I.9 he depicts his feebleness in being unable to shrug off the unwanted attentions of a social climber. In several poems in Book II he depicts himself at the mercy of individuals breaking in on his leisure to deliver second-hand Stoic sermons on madness and freedom at him—a bankrupt called Damasippus in Satire II.3 and his own slave Davus in II.7. Whether the real Horace was anything like this we cannot say, but it is clear that the poet uses this stance to create a disarming position from which to launch his criticisms of Roman morals and Roman society.

The logical corollary of his humble persona is his limitation of stylistic range and his aspiration to a certain linguistic purity. Horace expels the Greek words and other colorful vocabulary typical of Lucilius and instead develops the idea of satirical poetry as "conversation," preferring everyday vocabulary to high-flown poetic language. This fits his referring to his poems as *sermones* ("conversations") as well as *satura*. He describes his pieces as "a chatty sort of poetry" and often obscures or complicates the verse form with frequent enjambment. This is captured very well by Juster's handling of the heroic couplet.

The most obvious manifestation of Horace's milder form of satire is that his attacks are never on famous individuals, but instead on types, sometimes named, sometimes not. This makes his satire rather oblique. For example, Satire I.1. which takes as its theme people's discontentedness with their own situation in life, is essentially an attack on avarice without targeting any specific miser. Satires I.2 and I.3 are further attacks on human inconsistency, again with no single specific target. Horace attributes this mode of criticism to his father, whom he praises generously in Satire I.4 and again in I.6. He incorporates further praise into I.6 when he celebrates his patron Maecenas for valuing individual worth over birth. By the end of Book I, Horace has established a mild mode of satire, which reproves moral and social failings without savaging particular eminent individuals—an approach that he concedes in Satire I.10 may not have a wide appeal but which he hopes will win approval from Maecenas and his sophisticated circle of friends. He rightly characterizes his approach to satire early in the first poem of the book as a combination of truth and humor: *quamquam ridentem dicere verum / quid vetat? ut pueris olim dant crustula blandi / doctores, elementa velint ut discere prima* (I.1, ll. 24–26), which Juster acutely renders: "but can't we laugh when we reveal a truth / like teachers bearing treats who bribe a youth / so that he'll gobble up his ABCs?"

In the second book Horace's satirical method is even more oblique. In contrast with the first, where Horace at least points a cautious finger at human foibles and failings, following his father's practice of identifying positive and negative role models, in the second book he takes a back seat—or even disappears altogether—and cedes the floor to other speakers. The audience is left to figure out how seriously to take these speakers. We might listen closely to some of them, for example, the lawyer Trebatius in Satire II.1, who advises Horace on the risks and advisability of continuing to write satire. But when in II.5 we meet the prophet Tiresias advising Ulysses on the thoroughly Roman topic of making money through legacy-hunting, it is clear that Horace is having fun debunking Homer's characters by making them cynical and mercenary. In II.2 a sturdy rustic called Ofellus delivers a surprisingly long and eloquent speech urging moderation in matters of food, while in Satire II.4 the chic Catius, who reveals himself an obsessive fool, shares with Horace a lecture on fine gastronomy that he has just heard. These opposed opinions on food are reiterated in Horace's version of the fable of the City Mouse and the Country Mouse that he incorporates into Satire II.6, not spoken directly by Horace but put into the mouth of one of his country neighbors. But any inclination to read the fable straightforwardly, as praise of country living, is undermined by Horace's own admission earlier in the poem that he enjoys aspects of city life, especially his conspicuous association with Maecenas, which is "like honey." The second book ends with a satire on social climbing, in which an over-anxious host called Nasidienus is mocked for his attempts to impress Maecenas & Co., a poem that anticipates the prose satirist Petronius' memorable creation in his *Satyricon*, written nearly a century later, of the awful Trimalchio, an ex-freedman millionaire who positively tyrannizes his guests. It may seem that in Satire II.8 Horace finally delivers a personal attack—but in fact the whole incident is narrated to Horace by his friend Fundanius, a comic poet, to whom Horace gives the last word. We are left to decide for ourselves the extent to which Horace endorses Fundanius' mockery of the social climber.

Juster's new verse translation of Horace's *Satires* is most welcome; it attains a high level of accuracy both literally and in tone; in short, it is a delight to read. His decision to write in meter is bold and unusual—but it works, especially when read aloud, which is the way that the original Latin reached its audience, through the ear rather than the eye. Despite Horace's claim that his poetry resembles prose, the *Satires* certainly are poetry: Horace adapts conventional Latin word order to fit the hexameter and engages in a skillful play between form and content.

Juster's use of meter is a proper acknowledgment of the constraints imposed by the Latin hexameter. His choice of iambic pentameter allows a conversational feel, given the iambic tendency of everyday English diction. And his embracing of rhyme, while reminding us that this is poetry, captures the often light and witty tone of Horace's Latin. His achievement in creating rhymed poetry with a conversational feel—in which the clever enjambments are just as crucial as the clever rhymes—is comparable to that of Vikram Seth, whose acclaimed and often hilarious 1986 novel *The Golden Gate* is written entirely in sonnet form. There can be little doubt that Juster's translation is a milestone in the modern reception of Horace's *Satires*.

Book I

∾ Satire 1

Tell me, Maecenas, why no one's content
with either what they've done or fate has sent,
yet they applaud men taking other trails.
"O lucky businessmen!"
                              the soldier wails,
his body weighted down by age and shattered,   5
yet whenever southern winds have battered
his boat, a businessman will surely cry,

"Can't beat the army life! Don't you know why?
Two sides will clash, and in a flash you'll see
a sudden death or joyous victory."   10

A lawyer praises every hick with hoe
in hand who knocks at dawn as roosters crow;
that bumpkin hauled to town to pay his debts
swears city living is the best it gets.
To make a comprehensive list you'd need   15
a Fabius (or windbags of that breed).
In brief, here's my elusive bottom line:
suppose some deity would give a sign,
then say,
              "I'm here because your prayers are granted,
so you, the lawyer, will now be replanted   20
as a farmer—you, the soldier, made
into a business mogul. So, now trade!
. . .C'mon! Get *on* with it! Why stand so still?"

They would refuse, yet with a little will,
they could rejoice! Why wouldn't it be just   25

for Jove, in light of what we have discussed,
to puff his cheeks and angrily declare
he'll never be so quick to hear a prayer?
Of course, I will not slight my criticisms
with jokes, like those who write wry witticisms,   30
but can't we laugh when we reveal a truth
like teachers bearing treats who bribe a youth
so that he'll gobble up his ABCs?
So let us set aside frivolities
and face hard facts: that farmer plowing rocks,   35
that vet, that merchant no one can outfox,
those sailors boldly crossing every ocean—
they've taken on their burdens with the notion
that because they've saved more than they need,
their golden years are safely guaranteed,   40
just like that insect whom they imitate—
the diligent but tiny ant—whose freight
is carted in then stacked up overhead
because its future seems so filled with dread.
Still, when Aquarius darkens the year   45
as it begins its turn, the ant stays near
to home (wise creature!) drawing on its stash,
but as for *you*, no heat or snow, no flash-
floods, fires or wars could interrupt your quest
for wealth until your hoard exceeds the rest.   50

What is the benefit that you create
with gold and silver you accumulate
in vast amounts if you just bury it
while you're alone and scared? You gripe,
                                        "To split
it leaves a measly penny as my fraction."   55

But if you don't, what is your hoard's attraction?
Suppose a hundred thousand sacks of grain
come from your mill. Your stomach would remain
the size of mine; the outcome is the same
that it would be if somehow you became   60
a slave whose shoulders hoisted loads of bread—
your idle peers would be no less well-fed.

Moreover, if you live your life aligned
with Nature's laws, what difference can you find
between a hundred acres to be plowed   65
and ten times that amount? You cry out loud,

"But I prefer selecting what I please
from giant piles!"

                              Why praise your granaries
instead of bins if hoarding never offers
an improvement over modest coffers?   70
It is as if you needed just a cup
or jug of water, but you summoned up
the gall to say,
                    "I would prefer you took
my portion from a river, not a brook!"

When savoring what luxuries provide us,   75
we're swept downriver by the fierce Aufidus
along with all the flotsam that's nearby,
while he who longs for what can satisfy
his basic needs avoids those waves of mud
and does not perish when these rivers flood.   80
But many people, lured by false desire,
will then respond,
                         "You never can acquire
too much because you are what you possess."

What do you do with people who profess
such views?
                    Tell them to wallow in despair   85
since that's the lot they chose!
                                        I would compare
them to that Athens miser who, they say,
would mock his neighbor's gossip in this way:
"The peons always hiss, but when I see
my trunks of coins I shout, 'Hooray for me!'"   90

Dry-throated Tantalus just misses streams
that tease his lips—why do you laugh? It seems
that trading names would tell your story too.

You snore with moneybags surrounding you
and treat them with religious veneration   95
or an art collector's fascination!
Don't you realize what your money means,
what use it serves? Go purchase bread, some greens,
a bit of wine, and any other stuff
that worries people when there's not enough.   100
To lie awake half-comatose with fear
because bloodthirsty robbers might be near,
or flames, or slaves who try to rob you blind—
is that so great? For that I would not mind

if I remained among the destitute,   105
since if you're feeling chills from fever shoot
right through your body, or some injury
is keeping you in bed, who will there be
to sit with you, to get your lotions ready,
to call the doctor when you feel unsteady,   110
then ship you back to kids and other kin?
You would recover to your wife's chagrin—
and to your son's. You'll be despised by all,
by people whom you barely can recall:
friends, neighbors, children. Why does it amaze   115
you that when you indulge your greedy ways
nobody gives you love you never earned?
Or, when your schemes for winning love were spurned
by family that Nature sent your way,
wouldn't your efforts cause the same dismay   120
as if you gave your well-trained mule a crack
at racing stallions at the Campus track?

In short, be cautious as you get ahead,
and when you grow more wealthy, let your dread
of poverty decrease, and when you gain   125
what you are seeking, let it ease your pain
so that you won't be like Ummidius,
who was—put bluntly—so cupidinous
he had to guess his count of moneybags
yet was so cheap he dressed in servant's rags.   130
Until his final moments he would brood

about his risk of death from lack of food
until Tyndareus' boldest daughter,
a former slavegirl, used her axe for slaughter.

"Exactly what, then, are you urging on us?   135
Live like Naevius or Nomentanus?"

You keep on posing opposite extremes!
When I advise against your chintzy schemes,
I'm not suggesting throwing cash around;
there surely is a balance to be found   140
between Tanais and the family
by marriage of Visellus. There must be
measure in actions; bounds that do not change
define the moral only in their range.

So I return to where I first began,   145
and ask why greed does not allow a man
to be content, and why he has to praise
those taking other paths and mope for days
about the larger udder of a goat
his neighbor prizes, *then* has to devote   150
himself to serial oneupsmanship
(though with the unwashed masses he will skip
comparisons). In such a competition,
a richer fool keeps blocking your position
as when the chariots escape the gate   155
and thunder forward at a reckless rate;
in hot pursuit you'll find some charioteer
who doesn't worry who is in the rear.
In the same fashion, hardly anyone
confesses joy, and then, when life is done,   160
says goodbye like a guest who's had his fill.
But I have also overstayed, and will
not add a word so no one thinks I stole
from droopy-eyed Crispinus some dull scroll.

ᣔ Satire 2

The gangs of Syrian flute-girls, the shills
who sell exotic potions for our ills,
the bums, the actresses, the silly twits
and others of that ilk, indulge in fits
of grief about the late Tigellius   5
because, of course, he was so generous.
Here, at the opposite extreme, this guy
who dreads the spendthrift label, would deny
a tiny handout for a flat-broke friend
though it would make his chills and hunger end.   10
If you should ever ask this fellow what
(besides demands of his relentless gut)
could justify ransacking the estate
his noble forebears labored to create—
while he was sliding deeply into debt   15
by buying every trifle he could get—
he'll answer that he doesn't want to seem. . .
meanspirited or cheap.
       He wins esteem
from some, but others do not understand.

Fufidius, enriched by loans and land,   20
so dreads the label of a prodigal
that he quintuples fees on principal,
and when his debtors plunge toward deeper trouble,
his attempts to get paid back redouble.
He preys on teens whose togas are brand new;   25
when fathers leave, he takes an IOU.

On hearing this, who would not blurt out,
                                             "Lord,
he must provide *himself* a fair reward!"?

Much like the father in the Terence play
who suffered when he sent his son away,   30
you can't accept that he's his own worst friend.

If now you ask,
                "When *does* this story end?"

it's here; afraid of missteps they might take,
fools often make the opposite mistake.
Maltinus wears his tunic down real low,   35
while others hoist it high enough to show
their cocks and prove their lewd impertinence.
Refined Rufillus always reeks of mints;
Gargonius of goat. There isn't much
that's in-between. Some men will only touch   40
a woman if a prudish robe can swallow
her ankles; others won't unless they wallow
in whorehouse stench. When Cato recognized
a friend outside a brothel, he advised
with godly insight,
                    "That's commendable!   45
When lust engorges veins, it's sensible
for bachelors to descend into this den
instead of banging wives of married men."

Cupiennius, who likes vaginas pure,
responds,
          "Such praise I'd rather not endure!"   50

It's worth it—if you're someone who prefers
that great disasters strike adulterers—
to pay attention to their chronic stress
and how fresh grief disrupts brief happiness.
One fellow went up to his roof and jumped;   55
a second died from whippings; robbers thumped
another man while he was on the run;
some guy paid ransom; yet another one

was roughed up by a gang—and once a blade
left someone with his balls and prick filleted.   60
Mobs roar,
         "It's justice!!!"
                      Galba won't agree.

So why are baubles picked up cheap or free
(i.e., freedwomen) thought to be less risky?
They will make Sallustius as frisky
as any husband screwing on the side,   65
yet if he tried to be both dignified
and generous (so far as they don't clash
and he's unchecked by reason or his cash),
he'd give them adequate remuneration
and spare himself from shame and devastation.   70
Instead, relying on this single thing
he swells with pride and takes to posturing
because, he can declare,
                  "I'd never paw
a married woman!"

                  It's the same old saw
we heard once from Marsaeus, who we know   75
became the paramour of Origo
and gave that starlet his ancestral lands
while vowing,
                "May I never lay my hands
on wives of other men!"
                    But you have laid
both actresses and hookers, which has made
your name more tarnished than your balance sheet!   80
Are you content to take this part, yet cheat
yourself of credit for the role you play?
It harms you nonetheless; to throw away
one's reputation and inheritance   85
is always evil. What's the difference
between a matron and a white-robed miss?
The son-in-law of Sulla, Villius,
a wretch too smitten with nobility,
was punished harshly and repeatedly   90

by Fausta; he was always getting hit
or held at swordpoint for the fun of it,
and then deposited outside the gate
when Longarenus entered for a date.
Imagine someone stuck in such a bind   95
whose penis was inclined to speak its mind:
"What satisfies you? Do *I* ask to probe
the crotch beneath a consul's daughter's robe?"

And what would be his likeliest reply?
"Her father *is* a VIP. . ."

                 Just try   100
to get through thoughtfully and not confuse
what you should shun with what you want to choose.
Doesn't it matter if dissatisfactions
stem from circumstance or your own actions?
Don't give yourself a reason for remorse;   105
forget the matrons, for they are a source
of misery and evil that will keep
you from the benefits you ought to reap.
Although, Cerinthus, you may want to fight,
your emerald or gems that are snow-white   110
won't make the legs or thighs of women soften
or more fragile, and indeed it's often
a whore who has the more attractive odds,
for she may sell without the false façades
and openly display what is for sale;   115
if she has charm, she need not hype her tale
while cautiously concealing what is coarse.
It's the same way that kings will buy a horse:
they keep it covered as they check it out
so they will never be deceived about   120
the fragile hoof that often lurks below
the gorgeous body putting on a show
of tapered flanks, fine head, and arching neck.
Their ways are wise, so never make your check
of an exquisite body with the eyes   125
of a Lynceus, but don't scrutinize
the others like Hypsaea so you're blind

to any imperfections you should find.
"Oh *what* a leg! What *arms!*"

                         Your blather flows
while viewing shapeless hips, a pointed nose,   130
no waist to speak of, and enormous feet.
With someone's wife, your view is incomplete
except that you can see her face; unless
she is Catia, her long, flowing dress
will hide the rest. But if you go pursue   135
forbidden joys—as crazy people do—
a host of obstacles will block your way:
attendants, vehicles, beauticians, stray
"consultants," floor-length gowns, a shawl that flatters—
a thousand things that blind you to what matters.   140
The other way to go is free and clear;
in Coan silk her torso may appear
as if it's naked, so a gimpy leg
or ugly foot are features you can peg.
Why lose your money and deceive yourself   145
when merchandise is not yet on the shelf?
The playboy sings,
                    "The hunter tracks down hares /
through blinding snow, / but he no longer cares /
once they're brought low,"
                       and then analogizes:
"My passion is quite similar; it rises   150
above the easy prey to chase the birds
in flight."

           Could you conceive that any words
of poetry would ever help to free
your heart of longing, angst, or agony?
And wouldn't it be better to inquire   155
as to nature's limits on desire—
both joys that it allows itself to feel
and aches from want—so you can tell the real
from ether? When your throat is burning up,
would you drink only from a gilded cup?   160
When you are famished, is your only wish

to taste the most exotic fowl or fish?
When your groin's throbbing, and you have in hand
some servant boy or girl at your command,
and you can feel it's time to make your thrust,   165
would you prefer to burst from pent-up lust?
Not me! I like a lover who combines
low standards and convenience. If she whines,
"A little later," "Buy me something more,"
or "Maybe when my husband's out the door,"   170
as Philodemus says, then she is fit
for eunuch priests since his prerequisite
is she not cost a lot and never stall
whenever she is called. She should be tall
and fair, yet never try to look endowed   175
with greater gifts than nature has allowed.
When lying on our sides, she looks to me
like Ilia, or maybe she could be
Egeria—since any name will do.
I never have misgivings when we screw   180
for fear her husband's coming back to town
from business in the boonies to break down
the door as mongrels yap, the building shakes
with yelling, knocks, and clatter, and she wakes
up pale as death and scurries off. The maid,   185
her co-conspirator, then grows afraid
of being beaten and begins her screaming;
her guilty mistress worries he'll be scheming
to steal the dowry while I save my hide.
Barefoot and nearly naked, I decide   190
I should escape; I'm dreading litigation,
a pummeling or loss of reputation.
Whenever someone's nailed, his fate is cruel
(even if Fabius can bend a rule).

❦ Satire 3

All singers share this fault: among their friends
they won't perform, but music never ends
when everybody thinks it should be through.
Sardinia's Tigellius would do
that sort of thing. If Caesar, who could sway   5
a man with force, had asked for him to play
while pleading friendship and their fathers' bond,
he would have failed to make the man respond.
He'd belt out "Io Bacche" just for fun
from egg hors d'oeuvres until the fruit was done—   10
first in falsetto, then he would descend
to measures at the lyre's lowest end.
He vacillated. Often he would flee
as if escaping from the enemy;
more often he would creep along so slowly   15
it appeared that he was bearing holy
offerings for Juno. He was prone
to keep two hundred slaves, but then might own
as few as ten. He would give grand accounts
of kings and tetrarchs, then he would announce,   20
"A table with three legs, an oyster shell
that's filled with spotless salt, and, to repel
the icy cold, a toga (though it *may*
be coarse) are all I ask for."

                       So let's say
you gave this fellow who embodied thrift   25
a million in sesterces as a gift.

Although he was "content" with simple ways,
his pockets would be empty in five days.
Throughout the night he would remain awake,
then snore throughout the day without a break.   30
There never was a person so askew!

Somebody may now ask, "How about you?
Have you no faults?" Indeed, but not the same,
and maybe ones that are a bit more tame.
When Maenius decided to attack   35
the name of Novius behind his back,
somebody interrupted him with,
                                       "*Hey!*
Do you not know yourself, or do you say
you do not notice due to all your lies?"
"I'm no self-critic," Maenius replies.   40

It's silly and obscene, this egotism,
and it deserves your public criticism.
For your own shortcomings, your eyes will burn,
then blur when smeared with balm. Why do they turn
as clear as any eagle's or a snake   45
of Epidaurus when it's time to take
a look at how friends fail?—although what goes
around comes back again whenever those
who scrutinize your faults are these same friends:

"He *is* a bit pugnacious, and offends   50
the keener noses of the present day."

He may feel ridiculed when people say
he cuts his hair the way that bumpkins do,
his toga drags, and an ill-fitting shoe
keeps slipping off, but he's a decent guy—   55
you won't find someone better if you try,
and vast capacities may hide within
that fellow's unsophisticated skin.
Once finished, shake yourself to check if seeds
of evil in your nature or bad deeds   60
are sown within you; in neglected fields
we need to burn away the weedy yields.

Let's turn now to this subject: being blind,
a man who is in love can never find
his girlfriend's blemishes and may extol   65
her flaws, just like Balbinus and the mole
of Hagna. With our friends I wish we'd make
a reasonably similar mistake
and ethics labeled it accordingly—
for if a friend has some deformity   70
we should, like fathers with their kids, not shun
the handicap. A dad will name a son
who's crosseyed "Blinky." If he is as tall
as Sisyphus the Midget, he will call
the son "Small Fry." A bowlegged boy who limps   75
will be affectionately known as "Gimps"
and one with twisted anklebones who hobbles
unsteadily will win the nickname "Wobbles."
Somebody's tight with money? Let's just say
that he's "quite frugal." Does a man display   80
few signs of tactfulness or self-restraint?
Within his social crowd, he tries to paint
himself as "eager." Is somebody loud
and blunt? Let's call him "candid" and "uncowed."
Obnoxious? Let's relabel him "empassioned."   85
For me this practice shows how bonds are fashioned
and preserved once formed, and yet we turn
good habits on their head and foul an urn
that was pristine. When someone lives nearby
who is an unassuming, honest guy,   90
we'll call him "Ox" or "Sluggo." One who glides
past every obstacle and always hides
his naked flank from likely enemies
while life is churning with its jealousies
and innuendos will be labeled "fake"   95
or "too conniving"—never "wide awake"
or "shrewd"—though if a person's so sincere
(as I would think, Maecenas, I appear
to you so often) that he'll interject,
perhaps, with chitchat, as his friends reflect   100
or read, we say he's short on *savoir faire*.

Alas! Despite remaining unaware
of adverse consequences, we endure
this rule inflicted on ourselves! For sure,
there's no one born without some faults; the best   105
possess those less substantial than the rest.
As is fair, any worthwhile friend will balance
my deficiencies against my talents,
and if he wants my friendship, he'll place weight
upon my qualities that compensate   110
for my shortcomings—if, in fact, they do!
And if he is intending to pursue
my friendship, fairness means he must be weighed
upon that scale. No one should be dismayed
if he discovers pimples on a friend—   115
unless he wants his own warts to offend.
If absolution is what someone wants,
he should expect to grant the same response.
Moreover, since we can't completely weed
out violent rage and errors of that breed   120
for people stuck with their stupidity,
why couldn't Reason with validity
rely upon its weights and measurements
and match fair penalties to each offense?

Suppose a servant who had cleared a dish   125
had licked some lukewarm sauce and tried the fish,
and then suppose his master had replied
by ordering the slave be crucified.
Sane men would call him more delirious
than Labeo. How much more serious   130
and crazy would you call *this* violation?
A friend commits a minor provocation
which you must overlook or otherwise
be thought ungracious. You then demonize
him and avoid him like that man in debt   135
who stays the furthest distance he can get
from Ruso; once the dreaded Kalends come,
unless that debtor somehow finds a sum
of cash or loan, he's collared by the throat

and has to listen to each anecdote   140
that Ruso ever wrote. That friend may pee
upon your couch while on a drinking spree
or send Evander's cherished saucer flying
off the table. Is this or, when dying
of hunger, plucking chicken from your plate   145
a reason why a friend is second-rate?
What is my recourse if the fellow steals,
betrays my trust, or welshes on his deals?

When up against the truth, those who proclaim
that all transgressions are about the same   150
start hyperventilating. They deny
both instinct and tradition, and defy
expediency, which appears to be
the source of fairness and equality.
When brute-like men, a mute and lawless pack,   155
first crawled into the world, they would attack
each other with their fists and nails, and then
with clubs, to steal an acorn or a den,
and then eventually armaments
that were developed by experience   160
until they found the nouns and verbs that brought
their cries and stirrings into realms of thought.
Soon they were shunning conflict, fortifying
villages and making laws—denying
everyone the chance to pillage, loot,   165
or carry off their wives, since the pursuit
of cunts provoked the most horrific wars
before Helen, though history ignores
men slain by those who were more powerful
while they were blithely rutting like a bull   170
within his herd. If you decide to scan
the records of the history of man,
you will concede that we created courts
from fear of lawlessness. When nature sorts
out what is good, it cannot separate   175
what's just from unjust or what should create
aversion to a thing we should pursue.

Nor should logic make us think it's true
that all offenses are identical—
from picking someone's baby vegetable   180
to stealing sacred items in the night.
Let's use a scale imposing what is right,
so that we don't inflict the cruelest lashing
on someone who deserves a milder thrashing.
And if you cane a person who has earned   185
a fiercer whipping, I am unconcerned
since you will tell me theft that's surreptitious
is just the same as robbery that's vicious,
and that your scythe would level small and great
offenses (if we'd let you legislate).   190
If somebody is wise and well-to-do,
a shoemaker who makes the finest shoe,
and he alone is suave and king, then why
demand what's owned already?

                              The reply?
"You're missing what the father of our school,   195
Chrysippus, had intended as the rule!
If someone wise has never made a pair
of shoes or sandals he himself could wear,
that man is still a cobbler."

                              "How's that so?"
"It is just like Hermogenes; although   200
he's silent, he retains his great cachet
as singer and musician, the same way
that wily Alfenus, once he discarded
his tools and shut his shop, was still regarded
as a cobbler in the truest sense   205
that one who's wise displays more competence
than others in their fields of expertise,
and in this sense is king."

                              "The urchins seize
your beard, and if your 'sceptre' won't repel
the mob, it crowds and bumps you as you yell   210
and bluster back at them. O most sublime
of mighty kings, I will not take much time!

While you, as king, go bathing for small change
without a fawning aide except the strange
Crispinus, my good friends will not be stern   215
when folly makes me fail; for them in turn
I'll gladly brush off any travesty
and thrive uncrowned more than 'Your Majesty.'"

∿ Satire 4

Such poets as Cratinus, Eupolis,
and Aristophanes—and numerous
other proponents of Old Comedy—
were of this habit: if, deservedly,
somebody should be called out as a louse   5
or thief, a killer, or a cheating spouse,
they would not feel restrained as they applied
their brand. Lucilius wholly relied
on them; he'd copy them but rearrange
their feet and rhythms as the only change.   10
He was keen-witted and a keen-nosed guy,
though crude when giving poetry a try.
This was his flaw: convinced it was a feat,
he'd stand upon one foot as he'd complete
two hundred lines of verse in just one hour.   15
During this slog, you'd wish you had the power
of correcting what he was reciting.
He was a gasbag, lazy in his writing
(writing competently, anyway);
as for his mounds of verse, I am blasé.   20

Look! Here's Crispinus sneaking up to tease
me with a "deal":
                    "Go grab your tablets, please,
and I will grab mine. Let's arrange a place,
a time, and referees, and have a race
to see who writes the most!"

                              The gods were kind   25
in shaping me a poor and puny mind,

27

which rarely has much insight to express,
but as for you, go chase your happiness
and imitate the air enclosed within
a bellows struggling against goat-skin   30
until the iron softens in the fire!
How fortunate is Fannius, supplier
of his own books and busts, while what I write
goes unread, and I'm frightened to recite
in public for this reason: with my style   35
there are some people who will barely smile
since nearly everyone deserves *some* scorn.
Pick someone from a crowd! He'll be forlorn
from greediness or failures in his life.
This fellow's lusting for another's wife—   40
that guy for boys. The glint of silver captures
yet another fellow; bronze enraptures
Albius. Another's deals are done
from distant regions of the rising sun
to places heated by its evening rays.   45
Indeed, he's carried headlong through hard days
just like a whirlwind's dust, afraid to lose
his capital or profits he pursues.
This bunch is stupefied by verse, and scorns
the poets:
                    "He has hay upon his horns!   50
Stand back!"
                    If he stirs laughter, he won't spare
himself or friends, and he'll be thrilled to share
whatever he has scribbled on his sheets
with everybody beating their retreats
from a hot oven or a water trough,   55
including crones and slaveboys!
                                        Don't race off!
Come listen to a bit of my reply:
to start with, I do not identify
myself as a real poet. You'd opine
that it is not enough to write a line   60
in meter, and a person such as me
who writes a chatty sort of poetry

could never be regarded in your eyes
as a real poet. You would recognize
a person who is brilliant, with a mind   65
that is far more inspired and the kind
of voice that resonates. Based on that thought,
some doubted whether comic verses ought
to count as verse because they can't convey
great force and energy in what they say   70
or how they say it. Though arranged in feet
(unlike prose) that incessantly repeat,
it's still just prose.

     "And yet the father raves
because his spendthrift son who madly craves
his slutty girlfriend doesn't take a deal   75
to marry for a dowry that's unreal,
and shames himself by marching drunk through town
with torches though the sun is not yet down."

So would it be less acrimonious
with the late father of Pomponius?   80
Accordingly, it is inadequate
to write a line that is inanimate,
which, if examined closely, would portray
a father's rage exactly the same way
it happened in that play. As for all this   85
I'm writing now and what Lucilius
produced in times past, if you rearranged
the meter and the rhythm, and exchanged
our first and latest words "when dreaded War's
unlocking iron-studded gates and doors,"   90
a poet's broken parts would not be found.

Enough discussion! Someday I'll expound
on whether this is proper verse; I'll turn
for now to asking whether your concern
should be perceived as having any force.   95
With pamphlets in their hands and badly hoarse,
fierce Sulcius and Caprius police
the streets so frightened thugs will keep the peace,

but anyone at all whose hands were clean
and led a life of virtue could demean   100
the two of them. If, hypothetically,
you were to take on the mentality
of thieves like Birrius and Caelius,
I never would become like Caprius
and Sulcius. Why should I be that scary?   105
There is no shop or pillar that would carry
my small books so that Hermogenes
Tigellius and customers would seize
them with their sweaty paws, and I recite
just for my friends—and just to be polite—   110
not anywhere in any public space.
While at the baths or at the marketplace,
a lot of people like to perorate;
enclosures let their voices resonate.
This pleases fools, not those who want to see   115
some sentiment and musicality.

"You love inflicting pain," the people say,
"and choose to do it in a vicious way."
What causes you to hurl this allegation?
Which of my peers provides substantiation?   120
The man who knocks a friend behind his back,
who stands aside when enemies attack,
who seeks huge laughs and status as a jokester,
who can invent a tale to be a hoaxster
and who can never keep a confidence,   125
he's dark! Romans, maintain your vigilance
with him! When dining you will often find
three couches where twelve people have reclined
and in that group there is a single guest
who always loves to piss upon the rest—   130
except the host who waters down the wine—
though later he'll stop being so benign
once he is properly intoxicated
and all his private thoughts are liberated
by Liber, god of truth and liberties.   135
You, who "despise" blackhearted men as these,

yet still consider them kind, frank and witty,
do I appear intemperate or snitty
to you because I have been laughing, since
"refined Rufillus always reeks of mints;   140
Gargonius of goat"? So if you'd heard
some mention of corruption that occurred
involving someone called Petillius
Capitolinus, you would shill, as this
is what your habit is.
                "He's been a friend   145
and colleague since our childhood. He would lend
a hand when asked, and I am pleased to see
he's living in the city problem-free,
although, however, I am mystified
that he could beat the rap when he was tried."   150

This is pure bile, the octopus' ink;
I'll ban this vice from all I write and think,
and if, as in the past, I can declare
one thing about myself, it's this I swear:
if I am blunt, or overridicule,   155
you should apply to me a lenient rule.
The best of fathers would ingrain in me
the need to label immorality
with actual examples. When he tried
to teach me cheapness (being satisfied   160
with what he was providing me), he'd say,
"See how young Albius has thrown away
his life, and Baius knows financial woe?
A fine example why one mustn't blow
one's patrimony!"

             To excoriate   165
those slobbering for whores:
                        "Don't imitate
Scetanus!"

          To discourage hot pursuit
of married women who are dissolute
though these affairs are thought legitimate:

"Trebonius was found while doing it;   170
his name's not good."

        He'd say, "One who is wise
will always be inclined to theorize
about what's best to seek and to reject.
For me it is enough if I protect
the standards your forefathers have maintained   175
and if I keep your name and life unstained
while you still need me to remain on guard.
Once time has made your mind and limbs more hard,
you'll swim unaided."

        As a boy, he'd mold
me with remarks like these, and if he told   180
me to begin some kind of undertaking:
"There are good reasons for the choice you're making"
(as he exposed some person singled out
for his assessment).

        To create some doubt:
"Whenever so-and-so is under fire   185
from adverse reports, *must* you inquire
any further as to if this deed
produces shame and nothing that you need?"

Just as a neighbor's death will terrify
a housebound glutton who, afraid to die,   190
determines that he must improve his ways,
a young and fragile spirit often stays
away from vice when others speak their minds.
From this experience, I lack the kinds
of character deficiencies that cause   195
disasters (though I'm stuck with smaller flaws
you should forgive).
        Perhaps I'll be set free
to some extent by more maturity,
a candid friend or personal reflection
for I do not need more introspection   200
while on my couch or at the colonnade:
"*This* is more just."

    "If *this* decision's made,
I'll lead a better life."
      "*This* choice will go
down well with friends."
       "*This* move by so-and-so
was unattractive."
      "Would I ever make   205
this kind of unintentional mistake?"

These are the ideas that I bat around
with my lips sealed. When leisure time is found,
I play with paper for a little fun.
Of the small faults I mentioned, this is one,   210
and if you offer up the least resistance,
mobs of poets will provide assistance.
Since we dwarf your numbers, like the Jews
we'll offer membership you can't refuse.

∾ Satire 5

When I had left majestic Rome behind,
I took some modest lodgings I could find
in a town called Aricia; with me
was my dear colleague, the most scholarly
of Greeks, the rhetorician Heliodorus.   5
Once we left, the destination for us
was Appius' Market, a dense mob
of men off ships and hucksters out to rob
the public. Out of laziness, we split
the trip in halves, though you can travel it   10
in just one day; with pauses for relaxing
the Appian Way is nowhere near as taxing.

Once there, due to the water (which was vile)
I battled with my gut and twisted while
my colleagues dined. Night was about to place   15
its cloak of shadow on the world and lace
the sky with constellations. Slaves would cry
out to the sailors; sailors would reply
in kind:
        "This cargo has to go ashore!"
"Jam in three hundred there!"
                "Enough, no more!"   20

As they collected fees and reined an ass,
they let a total of an hour pass.
Mean-spirited mosquitos and the frogs
who kept on croaking loudly from their bogs
disrupted sleep. A sailor marinating   25

in wine far past its prime was serenading
a long-lost girl, and someone passing through
supplied some louder harmonizing too.
Before too long, the traveler would get
some sleep in and the groggy sailor let   30
his donkey out to graze, then tied a rock
onto the donkey's rein so he could knock
off for the night to snore.

                          At break of day
we saw the boat still wasn't on its way,
but then some nasty fellow from the ship   35
jumped off and grabbed a willow switch to whip
the ass and sailor on the back and head.
By ten we pulled in, and in waters fed
by you, Feronia the water-sprite,
we cleansed our hands and faces. When our light   40
late-morning meal was done, we made the crawl
three miles to Anxur, visible to all
upon its gleaming rocks. Once there, our plan
involved a meeting with that worthy man
Maecenas and Cocceius, who were sent   45
as envoys to resolve an incident
and help embittered friends to compromise.
I smeared black ointment on my swollen eyes.

While I still had my finger in my eye,
Maecenas and Cocceius happened by,   50
and with them was Fonteius Capito,
so sound that Antony will never know
a better friend. In a lighthearted state
the group abandoned Fundi's magistrate,
Aufidius Luscus, as people joked   55
about the tray of coals that left him smoked
and the pretentious toga that he wore
with purple stripes and borders proper for
a senator.

                 Next, totally worn down,
we stopped a while at the Mamurras' town.   60

Murena offered us a place to stay
and Capito the meals. When the new day
had dawned, our gratitude became complete
because at Sinuessa we would greet
Plotius, Varius, and Virgil, who   65
possess far brighter souls than others do;
for them I have the greatest dedication.
O what embraces and exultation!
Unless I'm going crazy, nothing measures
up at all to friendship's many pleasures.   70

A villa in Campania beside
the bridge would shelter us; we were supplied
with salt and wood by local functionaries
who must take it from their commissaries.
At Capua we let the donkeys take   75
off their pack-saddles for an early break.
Maecenas left to find some recreation;
Virgil and I chose some relaxation
since most ballgames used for exercise
are tough while battling one's gut and eyes.   80
Again we moved on, and were welcomed by
the well-stocked villa of Cocceius high
above the taverns down in Caudium.

Now, Muse, regale us, with a minimum
of verbiage, about the epic scene   85
between Sarmentus, that true libertine,
and Messius Cicirrus—tossing in
for both contestants background on their kin.
Messius was the product of a breed
of very well-known Oscans; she who freed   90
Sarmentus is alive today. Despite
their ancestors, both men had come to fight!
Sarmentus started off the repartee:
"You're like an untamed horse, I have to say!"
We laughed, and Messius tossed back his head   95
and shouted, "Guilty!" Then Sarmentus said,
"Dehorned, you threaten? What would you have done
before your mutilation had begun?"

(on his left side his hairy brow was marred
as a result of being badly scarred)   100
While mocking his Campanian disease
and face, Sarmentus made repeated pleas
for him to do the Cyclops shepherd-dance
(while adding that he had no need to prance
in shoes of tragic actors—or to use   105
a mask). Cicirrus then explained *his* views.
He asked Sarmentus why he would refrain
from offering the household gods his chain;
although he had become a scribe, the claim
his former owner had was "still the same."   110
His final flourish was to ask him why
he had escaped; one could satisfy
somebody puny and emaciated
with small amounts of gruel. Exhilarated,
we happily prolonged the whole affair.   115

We headed off to Beneventum, where
our fussy host came close to being toasted
as braces of his skimpy thrushes roasted
above the dying flames. As Vulcan flew
from kitchen walls, the fire blew right through   120
to lick the roof. You'd have seen everyone—
both starving guests and nervous servants—run
to grab the food and try to quench the blaze!

Apulia then made me fix my gaze
upon familiar hills that had been dried   125
by Atabulus; we would not have tried
to crawl across but for an invitation
to a villa near our destination,
Trivicum, whose smoky atmosphere
produced by burning saplings made us tear   130
up now and then. There, lacking any clue,
I waited for a midnight rendezvous—
except the lying girl did not arrive.
With my desires still on overdrive,
I nodded off. While sleeping on my butt,   135
a wet dream stained my nightshirt and my gut.

From this location we were hauled away
by carriage for two dozen miles to stay
the night in this small town I cannot name
in meter, but can show you just the same.   140
Here, water, nature's cheapest merchandise,
can be obtained, though only for a price,
but bread is so superb that tourists load
it high to have enough while on the road,
and at Canusium, the ancient city   145
of brave Diomede, their bread is gritty
(and their jugs of water aren't so cheap).
Here, as dejected friends began to weep,
Varius left.

        Exhausted by the strain
of grueling days on roads destroyed by rain,   150
we came to Rubi. Weather the next day
improved, but roads were worse along the way
to Barium, a walled-in fishing town.
Once we departed, we continued down
to Gnatia, constructed to annoy   155
the water-nymphs, where we would all enjoy
some jokes and snickering at the expense
of locals telling us that frankincense
melts on their temple steps without a flame.
The Jew Apella may believe this claim;   160
not I, for I have learned that deities
pass through their time without our miseries
and Nature's miracles are not hurled down
when gods above us in the heavens frown.

This lengthy narrative and journey come   165
to a conclusion at Brundisium.

～ Satire 6

Although no Lydian in Tuscany,
Maecenas, boasts a better pedigree
than yours, and on both sides your forebears led
vast legions, you don't snub those humbly bred
or freedmen's sons like me, as others do.   5
Whenever you declare that it's untrue
that you're concerned about a person's birth
(on the condition he's a man of worth),
you have convinced yourself that frequently
men lacking rank were living decently   10
and holding offices of high esteem
until the rise and infamous regime
of Tullius. Laevinus, to present
another countervailing precedent,
heir of Valerius (the inspiration   15
for ending haughty Tarquin's domination
and forcing him to flee), was vilified
and viewed as worthless under law applied
by popular opinion, which bestows
its most important offices on those   20
enthralled by fame and dazed by statuary
and inscriptions. So what's necessary
for us to do, who are far, far away
from common people? Let's suppose we say
it's true the people have a preference   25
for a Laevinus in their governance
instead of Decius with much to prove,
and Appius the Censor would remove

me from the Senate's list if it weren't true
I had a freedman father—rightly too,   30
considering the fact I haven't been
remaining reticent within my skin.
Still, Glory in its gleaming chariot
drags through the dust the proletariat
no less than noblemen. What have you earned,   35
Tillius, taking up the stripe you spurned
so you could be a tribune? Envy spread;
if you had chosen private life instead,
it would have been diminished. When we find
a person crazed enough that he will bind   40
his legs with those black leather straps and rest
an ample purple stripe upon his chest,
he hears before too long:
                              "Who *is* this guy?"
"He is the son of *whom*?"

                              If sickened by
the same disease as Barrus and aspiring   45
to be the beauty everyone's desiring,
wherever he may go he'll make the girls
debate details: face, calves, feet, teeth, and curls.
Likewise, those who protect the citizenry,
the city, the empire, Italy   50
and sacred temples of the gods inspire
all mortals to be eager to inquire
about paternity or someone's shame
that comes when mother lacks a well-known name.
Would you display the same decisiveness—   55
as heir to Dama, Dionysius
and Syrus—hurling citizens from high
off rock or bartering for them to die
with Cadmus?
                  "But a row behind me sits
Novius, one of my associates,   60
who's where my father was."
                              "You're thinking now
you're Paullus or Messalla?"

                                   Anyhow,
if at the Forum scores of wagons ran
into three giant funerals, this man
would swamp the horns and trumpets as he yelled;   65
at least by yelling our attention's held.

I come back to myself, a freedman's son,
who people snipe at as a freedman's son,
since now, Maecenas, I'm allied with you,
though as a tribune I was someone who   70
had led a legion. One cannot compare
these different things, for while it may be fair
begrudging me my post, one can't reject
our friendship, since you're careful to select
extremely worthy men who stay away   75
from self-promoting scams. I cannot say
that I was fortunate that happenstance
made you my friend because it was not chance
that put you in my path. Some time ago,
supremely gifted Virgil let you know   80
about me; Varius then did the same.
When we met face-to-face, my childish shame
led me to choke on words and lose my train
of thought before I went on to explain
just who I was, that I was not the son   85
of a distinguished father, and not one
who used his Saturean nag to ride
around his houses in the countryside.

As is your way, you made a brief reply.
I took my leave, and when nine months went by   90
you called for me again to indicate
I was to be among your friends. I rate
it as a compliment to be embraced
by you, who sort the good from evil based
not on a famous father, and instead   95
rely upon the life that one has led
and purity of heart. If, nonetheless,
despite some intermittent waywardness,
my character is otherwise alright

(just like somebody shrugging off the sight   100
of a great body with some minor warts);
if there are no reliable reports
accusing me of mean or greedy ways,
or whorehouse trips; and if, to overpraise
myself, I live a life of circumspection   105
and modesty, and have my friends' affection,
then it would be just as my father planned,
because, though poor, with only meager land,
he was unwilling to dispose of me
in Flavius' school, where there would be   110
those loutish scions of centurions
with each one carrying eight bits of bronze
for his tuition payments on the Ides
and swinging slates and bags on their left sides,
and yet he had the pluck to take his son   115
to Rome for education as it's done
for children of a senator or knight.
If anyone had ever seen the sight
of me with fawning slaves and fancy clothes
(in the big-city style) he would suppose   120
a family estate had paid my way.
A flawless guardian, he'd always stay
with me when teachers wanted me alone.
What else is necessary to be shown?
He saved my innocence (which is the state   125
out of which virtue may originate)
from vice and shameful things that people say,
and didn't worry that someone someday
would criticize him if I ever made
the small commissions of the crier's trade   130
or, as he did, those of an auctioneer.
Nor do I have complaints; for me it's clear
I owe him greater praise and gratitude.
While of sound mind, I'll take the attitude
of having no regrets about a father   135
of this type, and therefore will not bother
to defend myself, as many do,
relying on the customary view

that we are spared responsibility
for parents who don't have a pedigree   140
or great accomplishments. My argument
and logic are completely different.
If Nature, at some age, were to direct
us to retrace our paths, and to select
replacement parents based upon our pride,   145
my own would keep me fully satisfied
and I'd refuse to pick somebody known
as noble by his scepter and his throne.
I may be crazy in the public's view,
though maybe I'm appearing sane to you,   150
because this is a burden I won't bear
since right away I'd feel compelled to scare
up lots of money, do more socially;
for traveling abroad or locally
I'd need "associates"—at least a few;   155
I'd feed more horses, and their trainers too,
and lead a line of carts. Now, if I want,
I'll take my gelded mule out for a jaunt
into Tarentum though his back may break
from lugging saddlebags, and his flanks ache   160
from lugging me. Nobody hurls at me,
Tillius, charges of vulgarity
which was the problem when you took the road
to Tibur—as the praetor—with commode
and wine containers carried by five boys.   165
In this regard my life has greater joys
than yours, great senator, and thousands more.

When I am in the mood, I go explore
entirely alone and ascertain
the prices set for vegetables and grain.   170
As evening falls, I often wander through
the sketchy Circus and the Forum too.
I stand beside astrologers, then troop
back home to have some leek and chickpea soup.
Three slaveboys serve my meals, and polished stone   175
supports the ladle and two cups I own.

Beside these items is some bric-a-brac
made in Campania: a cheap knick-knack,
an oil-flask with its dish. When supper's done,
I sleep unworried that I'll need to run   180
out for an early meeting or appear
in front of Marsyas (who is quite clear
that looking at the face of Novius
the Lesser should be viewed as odious).
I lie in bed till ten, then take a stroll,   185
or read or write a piece I think is droll.
I rub myself with oil, but not the type
from lamps that grubby Natta likes to swipe,
though when I get worn down and fiercer sun
reminds me I should go and bathe, I shun   190
the ballgames and the Campus. Lunch is light,
enough so I don't starve before the night;
I stay at home and putter lazily.

This is the life of anybody free
of burdensome, depressing aspirations.   195
These things provide me with the consolations
of a life more pleasantly employed
than what my grandfather would have enjoyed—
my father and my uncle in addition—
had they gained a senator's position.   200

∽ Satire 7

Reports about that mongrel Persius,
who took revenge upon the merciless
and venomous Rupilius "the King,"
an outcast, are old news for gossiping
hairstylists and the slackers with red eyes.   5
This Persius, a man of enterprise,
was dealing with a business operation
at Clazomenae and some litigation
with "King" as well. He was a crusty sort,
so thoroughly obnoxious he could thwart   10
the "royal" will, so overbearing, flip
and caustic that his verbal jabs could zip
past Barrus or Sisenna like white steeds.

So, back to "King." When no approach succeeds
with Persius since rivals must embrace   15
the hero's right to battle face-to-face
(much as it was with Hector, Priam's son,
and brave Achilles, where their rage had run
so high), the only option that remained
for backing off was death, a fact explained   20
by peerless valor. With hostilities
between two cowards or with enemies
unequal in their strength, like Diomede
and Lycia's Glaucus, the weak recede
and sometimes send "a token of esteem."   25
Rupilius and Persius—a team
like Bacchius and Bithus—rush to court

to offer evenly contested sport
during this period when Brutus reigns
as Asian praetor. Persius explains   30
his case so poorly that the people laugh;
he warmly praises Brutus and his staff.
"The Asian sun" becomes his appellation
for Brutus; for his aides "a constellation
of guiding stars"—except for "King," who "came   35
on like The Dogstar," a much-hated name
among the farmers. His remarks careen
like torrents racing through a cold ravine
in virgin forest spared the woodman's axe.
Then, in response to floods of witty cracks,   40
the fellow from Praeneste spits replies
just like the vulgar taunts of vineyard guys
who seem imposing to the tourists who
are nervous but keep hooting out "Cuckoo!"
But Persius the Greek, drenched bitterly   45
by now with vinegar from Italy,
cries, "Brutus, by the mighty gods I pray,
since regicide is on your résumé,
why don't you get ahead with this 'King' too?
Trust me, a job like this is made for you!"

∾ Satire 8

In days gone by, I was a fig-tree trunk,
a piece of wood that was considered junk,
until the carpenter, who was divided
between Priapus and a stool, decided
I was to be a god.
           So I became   5
a god, the scourge of thieves and birds. I tame
the thieves with a right hand prepared to strike
intruders and a scarlet wooden spike
lasciviously jutting from my groin,
while those annoying birds refuse to join   10
me in this brand-new park because they dread
the flapping reed that's fastened to my head.
Here slaves once had to buy a discount bier
to haul away the people they held dear
whenever corpses were evicted from   15
their tiny cells. Here's where the poor would come
for burial, from spendthrift Nomentanus
to the parasitic Pantolabus.
Here pillars mark the limits on each side—
a thousand feet across, three hundred wide—   20
and tell the passers-by this sanctuary
will never pass to heirs.
                Now the unwary
fill a healthy Esquiline and stroll
upon the sun-drenched rampart; not a soul
can see the bleaching bones within this ground.   25
For me, the thieves and creatures I have found

do not concern me anywhere as much
as witches with their drugs and spells who touch
the spirit with malevolent intent;
there isn't any way I can prevent   30
collection of some bones or poison plants
whenever the unsettled moon enchants
us with her graceful face. I testify
I've seen Canidia—black robe hiked high,
without her shoes, her hair a tortured mess—   35
out howling with the ancient sorceress
Sagana. When the two of them appeared,
their pallor made them hideous and weird.
They started clawing up the dirt and chewing
on a mournful lamb whose blood was spewing   40
into a ditch so that they could release
the dead to answer them. With them were fleece
and waxen dolls; the larger of the pair—
the fleece one—had a dominating air.
The wax one cringed, as if it slavishly   45
awaited death. One witch called Hecate;
the other cruel Tisiphone. You might
have witnessed snakes and hellhounds on this site,
and the moon blushing with a blood-red shade
behind tall tombs so that it could evade   50
these horrors.
                        If I lie—even a bit—
may ravens dump their alabaster shit
upon my head, and then may Julius,
fey Pediatia and scurrilous
Voranus piss and crap all over me!   55
I'll skip details, such as how chillingly
and mournfully the demons summoned by
Sagana gave her questions their reply;
how they both slyly buried some wolf-beard
and fang of speckled viper; how flames reared   60
when the wax image burned; and how, as one
who saw it all, I shook at what was done
and said by these two Furies, upon whom
I took revenge. By farting with a BOOM

like bursting bags, my figwood backside split;   65
the witches ran to town. Amid our wit
and laughter, you'd have seen, if you were there,
Canidia's false teeth and phony hair
Sagana wears up high as it all tumbled
down with charms and potions that they fumbled.   70

❧ Satire 9

As I was strolling down the Sacred Way
for no real reason, pondering some stray
idea with the utmost concentration,
this fellow whom I know by reputation
comes running up and grabs my hand.   "So how   5
are you, dear friend?"
                    "Quite well. . .until just now,"
was my reply.
            "I wish you all the best!"

As he continues being quite a pest,
I snap,
        "What is it *now*?"
                        and he's complaining,
"You must know me—I've had first-class training!"   10

so I say,
        "I'm *horribly* impressed!"

To shake this boor who's making me distressed,
I walk more quickly, then abruptly veer
away and whisper in my servant's ear
as streams of sweat cascade onto my feet.   15
I murmur, "Oh Bolanus, what a treat
to have your temper!" as the boor heaps praise
on every precinct in so many ways
he praises Rome in its entirety.

When I do not respond, he lectures me,   20
"You're in an awful hurry to break loose.
I've noticed that in you—but it's no use.
I'll stand beside you all along the way!"

"There *really* is no need for you to stay.
I want to visit someone you don't know;   25
he's sick in bed, and I will *have* to go
across the Tiber near the parks of Caesar."

"I'm not engaged in anything but leisure,
and I'm not sluggish; I will follow you."

I drop my ears as sullen donkeys do   30
when overloaded. He begins to sell
with, "If I have done my self-assessment well,
when choosing friends, you should evaluate
me as somebody you'd appreciate
far more than Varius and Viscus, for   35
who cranks out verse as quickly? Or much more?
Who moves with greater grace? Hermogenes
himself would envy my sweet melodies!"

I have to break in.
                            "Do you have a mother
who must be supported? Or another   40
relative?"
              "Nobody. I have laid
them all to rest."
                      "What luck for them! I've stayed
behind, so finish me off as I near
who, in my boyhood, saw my destiny
by shaking urns, and sang these lines to me: 45

No poison herb or hostile sword will slay him;
nor TB, whooping cough or gout will dismay him.
A blabbermouth will suck the air around him;
he must avoid a gasbag who will hound him."   50

Having consumed a quarter of the day
already, both of us then make our way

to Vesta's temple, where by accident
he learns he'll forfeit to a litigant
if he does not officially appear   55
in court for his defense. "Assist me here
a little if you are my friend!" he pleads.

"Damn me if I possess what someone needs
to testify or understand our laws!
I have to hurry off, you know the cause."   60

He says, "I wonder what I ought to do—
should I abandon my response or you?"

"Me please!"

                    "I shall not do it!" he replies.

Because it's risky to antagonize
a person who you know you just can't whip,   65
I follow him.
                    "Is your relationship
good with Maecenas?"

                              He begins again,
". . .a man who has few friends, but acumen.
Nobody's wiser when he makes a bet.
If you would introduce me, you would get   70
an ardent advocate, a number two.
Damn me if there's someone we won't outdo!"

"The way we're living there is different
from what you think; our group's more innocent
and free of vices. I'm not agitated   75
if someone's richer or more educated.
Each to his own."
                         "That's quite a tale you weave,
although it is not easy to believe."

"Yet, nonetheless, it is the truth."
                                        "You fire
me up with even more intense desire   80
to be his confidant!"

                                                      "You can express
your interest; with all your manliness
I'm sure you can prevail. You can rely
on him to drop his guard, which tells you why
it's hard to get a meeting with the man."   85

"I will not be deflected from my plan!
I'll bribe his slaves! If first I fail, I'll fight
and never stop! I'll find the time that's right!
I'll chase him through the public squares! I'll go
accompany him! 'Life does not bestow   90
its benefits on man without hard work.'"

As he continues acting like a jerk,
Aristius Fuscus, my cherished friend,
who knows him full well, comes around the bend.
We take a break. He asks, "Where have you been?"   95
and "Any plans?" then chatters. I begin
to tug upon his toga and to prod
his unresponsive arm, then wink and nod
for rescue. Joking with an evil twist,
he smirks and keeps pretending he has missed   100
what's going on. I'm getting steaming mad.

"I'm *positive* you told me that we had
a matter for *discreet* consideration."

"I do recall. We'll have that conversation
at a better moment. With today   105
the thirtieth—the Sabbath—would you say
something offensive to the dock-tailed Jews?"

I say, "I hold no superstitious views."

"Not so for me. I am a bit more weak,
part of the crowd. Forgive me, we will speak   110
some other time."
                        To think so bleak a sun
is hanging over me! The shameless one
escapes and leaves me on the edge. By chance,
he meets his plaintiff face-to-face, who rants,

"Where are you going now, you piece of scum?"   115
then turns to me to ask, "Will you become
my witness?" Then I let him touch my ear;
they're off to court. Loud shouts are all I hear,
and crowds race everywhere without direction
(Apollo's way of giving me protection).   120

∿ Satire 10

I did make comments, undeniably,
stating Lucilius's poetry
stumbles on clumsy feet. Which advocate
of his, however foolish, won't admit
this view is true? At least he got some praise   5
on the exact same page for all the ways
he spiced up Rome! I'll grant he passed that test,
but see no reason to concede the rest
because Laberius's vulgar shows
would then be pretty verse. Plays such as those   10
do have some value, but we need much more
than simply making audiences roar.

You need to be concise, so that a thought
can run on without ever being caught
in bombast battering our weary ears.   15
You also must create a style that veers
from grave to giddy, runs from lyrical
to lofty, and can be satirical,
while limiting your zeal and holding back
your point of view. A joke can often hack   20
through knotty problems more emphatically
than something stated diplomatically.
With this approach, the famous men who wrote
Old Comedy accomplished much of note,
and so let's imitate such men as these—   25
those writers whom that fop Hermogenes
has never read—but not that trained baboon

whose only claim to fame is that he'll croon
some Calvus and Catullus. Some may plead
that melding Greek and Latin was a deed   30
of genius. . .O you dopes! Why do you rate
what little he has done as something great
or startling? And yet when I proclaim
Pitholeon of Rhodes did just the same,
you say it's sweeter when the words combine   35
like mixed Falernian and Chian wine.
So, I must ask you, does this rule apply
just for composing verse, or does it fly
when you defend Petillius in court
with lousy arguments of last resort?   40
While Pedius and Publicola sweat
about their legal briefs, would you forget
Father Latinus and your fatherland
by bastardizing speech we understand
with foreign imports like the verbal fusions   45
found in argot spoken by Canusians?
Though born upon these shores, I used to write
my verse in Greek, but once, deep in the night
when dreams are true, I heard Quirinus speak
this warning:
                    "Giving us another Greek   50
is like transporting timber to the trees."

So while that pillar of pomposities,
Alpinus, takes his blade to Memnon's throat
and dams the Rhine's headwaters, I devote
myself to fluff that nobody will hear   55
at Tarpa's Temple games and won't appear
in multiple revivals on the stage.
Fundanius, of poets of this age,
only you please us with that repartee
of Davus and the crafty whore who play   60
old Chremes for a fool. Pollio sings
about the noble victories of kings
in triple meters. Varius, far more
than others, stirs us with his tales of war.

The Muses, who intended to express   65
the joys of country life, gave gentleness
and wit to Virgil. Satire was a test
that Varro Atacinus and the rest
have failed, and though I managed to succeed,
I pale beside the pioneer. Indeed,   70
the crown of glory resting on his head
is one I could not nudge—though I have said
his flow gets mucked up; downstream you can find
the garbage you would rather leave behind.

C'mon! I ask you: does your scholarship   75
suggest that Homer never made a slip?
Were tragedies of Accius so great
that suave Lucilius would hesitate
to make some changes? Didn't he have fun
when lines of Ennius were crudely done,   80
while for himself he wasn't one who claimed
to be superior to those he blamed?
So when we read Lucilius, why be
afraid to ask if his ability
or the great difficulty of his themes   85
is what denied him poetry that seems
less polished and melodic in its flow
than poetry of someone who can throw
his every thought into a six-beat line
and then, believing this approach is fine,   90
delights in cranking out two hundred more
both after eating dinner and before?
The Tuscan Cassius was of that breed—
worse than a torrent churning at high speed—
and for his funeral they lit a fire,   95
then used his books and shelves to fuel his pyre.
Granted, Lucilius was both urbane
and suave. Granted, his satires did attain,
surprisingly, more style than one might see
from one who wrote ungraceful poetry   100
untainted by the Greeks or delegations
of poets from the older generations—

and yet, if fate could put him here today,
he would revise far more and hack away
at excess verbiage, then scratch his head   105
and chew his nails. For verse to be reread,
you must be willing to invert your stile,
remain above the crowd, and reconcile
yourself to unread work—or, like a fool,
do recitations at some awful school.   110
Not me! As brash Arbuscula would sneer,
"I'll take the boos of clods if knights will cheer."
Why should I let myself get aggravated
by that louse Pantilius or bated
by Demetrius, who snipes at me   115
at every chance (though never frontally),
or smeared by vapid Fannius, that sleaze
who always mooches off Hermogenes
Tigellius and acts in nasty ways?

Let Plotius and Varius heap praise   120
upon my verse as well as Valgius,
Maecenas, Virgil—plus Octavius
and Fuscus, who are finer men than others—
and, in addition, both the Viscus brothers!
I could identify, without a show   125
of any flattery, you, Pollio;
Messala, you as well—your brother too;
you, Bibulus and Servius, and who
except you, candid Furnius, and more
old friends and scholars. . .whom I must ignore.   130
I hope my verse, such as it is, brings joy
to all of them because it will annoy
me if my well-laid plans start falling through.
Demetrius, Tigellius: you two
can sit through class so schoolgirls hear your whines.   135
Run, boy! In my small book, go add these lines.

Book II

◟ Satire 1

HORACE: "There is a group that claims my satire seems
   too harsh and crosses lines in ways it deems
   improper. Others call it 'slack' and say
   that anyone could crank out in a day
   my thousand lines. How should this be addressed,   5
   Trebatius? Decide."

TREBATIUS: "Give it a rest."

HORACE: "You mean. . .stop writing verse?"

TREBATIUS: "That's what I feel."

HORACE: "May I be ruined if that's not ideal—
   but I *can't* rest."

TREBATIUS: "Let those who need deep sleep
   get rubbed down, do three Tiber swims, and keep   10
   themselves, until the evening, marinated
   in lots of wine that's unadulterated,
   or if you're captivated by a passion
   for composing verse, then dare to fashion
   tales describing mighty Caesar's actions;   15
   your labors will produce great 'satisfactions.'"

HORACE: "Most wise advisor, that's my aspiration,
   but I do not have the motivation;
   some just can't paint an image that recalls
   troops bristling with javelins or Gauls   20
   expiring when impaled by splintered spears

or some hurt Parthian whose stallion rears
and throws him."

TREBATIUS: "Yet you still could represent
    his bold and even-handed temperament,
    like wise Lucilius with Scipio."   25

HORACE: "I will not stray from where I need to go—
    when it is time. Until that time is here,
    the words of Flaccus slide by Caesar's ear,
    and if you stroke him in the wrong direction,
    he will lash back for his own protection."   30

TREBATIUS: "How much more practical that choice would be
    than slamming with acidic poetry
    a person such as 'spendthrift Nomentanus'
    or 'the parasitic Pantolabus'
    when everybody's fending off alarm   35
    and hating you—although they've felt no harm! "

HORACE: "What can I do? Milonius will rise
    to dance as soon as heat intensifies
    in his wine-clobbered brain and lamps divide
    in pairs. For Castor, horses are his pride   40
    and joy; his twin, who shared his egg when hatched,
    prefers it when two boxers have been matched.
    As with Lucilius, a man far better
    than us both, my pleasure is to fetter
    words in feet. In days of long ago,   45
    he poured his secrets into books as though
    they were good friends; he had no other source
    of help when things went well or far off course.
    The old man's life was openly displayed
    as if a votive tablet scene had laid   50
    it out quite clearly. I'm a partisan
    of him, but whether I'm Lucanian
    or more Apulian is hard to say,
    for in Venusia an émigré
    plows fields on borders near both territories.   55
    As reported in the musty stories,

once the Samnites were expelled, Rome sent
in colonists so that it could prevent
attacks by enemies through vacant land
no matter if the threats of war were planned   60
by tribesmen of Apulia or by
Lucanians—and yet this pen will shy
from groundless jabs at people still alive,
and it will even help me to survive.
As with a sheath that's wrapped around a blade,   65
why should I wield it when I'm unafraid
of vicious thugs? O Jupiter, my Lord
and Father, lay aside my rusty sword
and shield peace-loving me, though anyone
who riles me will regret what he has done   70
(it's better not to touch me, I declare!)
and will be scorned and slandered everywhere
around the city! Where there's provocation,
Cervius will threaten litigation
and the jurors' urns; for enemies   75
Canidia has lethal remedies
she uses that Albucius provides;
if you're in court when Turius decides,
he'll come down hard! Since everyone relies
upon his strongest weapon when he tries   80
to frighten those he fears, you must allow—
as I have always done—that this is how
almighty Nature reigns; the wolf will use
its fangs; the bull its horns. How do they choose
behaviors if they're not intuitive?   85
If Scaeva's mother, who intends to live
forever, is entrusted to the care
of her free-spending son, he'd never dare
to lift his trustworthy right hand to treat
a person badly (a surprising feat,   90
like wolves who won't attack you with their claws
or oxen who refuse to use their jaws).
In any case, some poisoned honey rich
with lethal hemlock will undo the bitch.

In short, regardless if the future brings   95
me Death that's circling on sable wings,
a calm retirement, financial need,
the open air of Rome—or, if decreed
by Fortune—exile, but however bright
or dull my life becomes, I will still write!"   100

TREBATIUS: "O lad, your life—and sidekicks who will freeze
    you out—keep giving me anxieties!"

HORACE: "What? When Lucilius first boldly tried
    some verses of this type, and stripped the hide
    off those who, while in public, liked to preen   105
    in spite of being inwardly obscene,
    were Laelius or he who earned his name
    by crushing Carthage feeling any shame
    due to his talents? Were they greatly pained
    by damage that Metellus had sustained   110
    or Lupus being swamped by vitriol
    in verse? Yet he excoriated all
    the people's tribal clans and leaders, though
    no doubt the only kindness he would show
    was what he showed to Virtue and to men   115
    who loved it. For indeed, at moments when
    brave Scipio would join the gentle sage
    called Laelius and fled the public stage
    and crowds for private places, they would play
    around with him and wile away the day   120
    with tunics loose so they could have some fun
    until their simmered vegetables were done.
    Whatever I may be, although I lack
    Lucilius' property and knack
    for writing, Envy still can't hesitate   125
    conceding I have lived among the great
    and, while pursuing something soft to chew,
    will break her tooth on something hard, if you,
    well-versed Trebatius, do not dissent."

TREBATIUS: "Indeed, I have no counterargument,   130
    but you're on notice, which should give you pause,

since lack of knowledge of our sacred laws
can bring you trouble. If a person slights
another with vile verses, there are rights
of action he can use and remedies."   135

HORACE: "Sure, if they're vile. . .What if they're good and please
the critic Caesar? Say he barks at one
who earned abuse, while he himself earned none?"

TREBATIUS: "They'll wipe all your official records clean,
and laugh as you, unpunished, leave the scene."   140

ᘒ Satire 2

HORACE: "*The Definition and the Benefits*
of Simple Living.
                    Dear associates,
this isn't yet another of *my* speeches—
it's what that unschooled sage Ofellus teaches
as his rustic wisdom:
                    'Educate   5
yourself, but not amid the silver plate
and tables where a person could go blind
from crazy glitziness and where the mind
will tend toward self-deception and reject
the opportunities it should select.   10
While lunchless, seek the truth with me right here.'"

ANONYMOUS FOIL: "Why do that?"

HORACE: "If I can, I'll make it clear.
A judge who is corrupt is never fair
about truth. After you've been hunting hare,
or coming back exhausted since your horse   15
was very difficult to keep on course,
or acting Greek in Roman martial drills
or rapid-action ballgames where the thrills
ease hardships so they're easier to do,
or discus throwing has inspired you   20
to throw a thing through yielding air, or stress
has bludgeoned out of you your fussiness,
and you are hungry and your throat is dry,
go on, don't think to give cheap food a try!

Don't drink the mead unless it's constituted   25
from Hymettan honey and diluted
with Falernian!
           And so let's say
your butler's on vacation for the day,
and fish are sheltered by the darkened seas,
you could rely on salted bread to ease   30
your growling gut. From where and how was *this*
discovered? You will find the greatest bliss
in your own self, not in expensive scents!
Earn sauce through sweat! The man whose decadence
has made him pale and bloated cannot love   35
his oysters, parrotfish or foreign dove!
Moreover, if a peacock's on your plate,
it won't be easy to eliminate
your urge to swab your tongue with it instead
of with some chicken, for you've been misled   40
by hollow things because odd birds are sold
for gold and, with plumes spread, they make a bold
display (as if that mattered). Do you eat
those feathers that you praise? Now that it's meat,
does it retain its grace? And yet, relying   45
on distinctions in their looks, you're dying
for the peacock—though the meat's the same!
Alright, but how can you support your claim
to tell a Tiber bass that strains to breathe
from those that come from where the currents seethe   50
below the bridges or the boundary
between the Tuscan river and the sea.
You praise a three-pound mullet, idiot,
although you always have to divvy it
up into single servings. In my view,   55
it is appearance that is hooking you.
Why, then, are lengthy bass so much despised?
Surely, the cause is nature has devised
that they be long, and mullets low in weight.
Only a rarely hungry gut can hate   60
a simple diet!

'But a giant fish
that is displayed upon a giant dish
is something I would really like to see!'
insists some glutton who deserves to be
among voracious Harpies!

                  And yet still,   65
you opportune Siroccos, may you grill
this food since turbot, though quite fresh, and boar
already reek, and eating any more
than usual upsets a queasy gut;
whenever guts are full but spot a glut   70
of food, they will prefer some bitter roots
and radishes. There are no substitutes
for pauper's food at banquets where kings reign;
today black olives and cheap eggs retain
their place. The sturgeon of the auctioneer   75
Gallonius have lately made men sneer.
Why? Were there fewer turbot in the sea?
Stork chicks and turbot had security
until some praetor educated you!
Thus, if some 'expert' edict said it's true   80
that roasted seagull was delectable,
the youth of Rome (who are susceptible
to learning evil lessons) would obey.
Poor diet, if Ofellus has his way,
must be distinguished from a plain cuisine,   85
for you won't dodge this vice if you careen
abruptly down that crooked avenue.
Avidienus, known as "Doggy" due
to actual behavior, feeds himself
just olives rotting five years on the shelf   90
and cornels from the woods, and will decline,
until it's turned, to open up his wine.
As for his oil, it's tough to tolerate
the stench. Though garbed in white to celebrate
a wedding, birthday, or some other feast,   95
he grabs a two-pound jug so that the least
amount of oil will drizzle just a bit

upon the greens, while being profligate
with ancient vinegar. So, of these takes
on life, which is the choice a wise man makes?   100
As such, he's cornered in a hopeless way
'between the wolf and dog,' as people say.
He'll have enough refinement to eschew
the world's vulgarity and not pursue
a wretched style of life through either route,   105
nor be, like old Albucius, a brute
when giving work to servants, nor provide
his guests with greasy water, as was tried
by lazy Naevius. This, too, should be
regarded as a huge deficiency.   110

Now listen to how simple eating brings
us all so many and such wondrous things!
First is good health because it's manifest—
as you recall plain fare you could digest—
that it's quite dangerous when foods collide.   115
Whenever you combine the boiled with fried,
or shellfish with a thrush, the sweet will turn
to bile, and clogging phlegm makes stomachs churn.
Don't people at a 'dinner served with doubt'
appear quite pale as they are coming out?   120
Moreover, overkill of yesterday
that drags a body down will also weigh
upon a soul and bury what's divine
within the ground. If someone can combine
nursing his limbs and falling off to sleep   125
without delay, he'll rise alert and keep
up with his obligations, even though
occasionally he may try to go
for something better if the passing year
brings feasting, or his wasting's so severe   130
that he intends to fix his malnutrition,
or, as time flies by, his frail condition
in old age requires gentler care.
But as for you, if you are forced to bear
enfeeblement from aging and disease,   135

how will you bolster your infirmities
once you have blown your youthful, healthy days?
Our ancestors were generous with praise
for rancid pork—not that they lacked a nose,
but based upon this thinking, I suppose: 140
if someone showed up for dinner late,
it was more fitting that he have a plate
of tainted ham than let the host feel free
to eat the boar in its entirety.
If only I could have arranged my birth   145
to join these heroes of primeval Earth!

You are a person who appreciates
a reputation, for it captivates
a person's ear more sweetly than a song,
but turbots on big platters go along   150
with scandals and financial devastation.
Add a mad uncle, neighbors, flagellation
of yourself, and thoughts of suicide
that were in vain since you could not provide
a penny for a noose.   'It's fine to pick,'   155
he says, 'on Trausius with rhetoric.
I have huge revenues and wealth three kings
would call enough!'
                        So aren't there better things
to spend your profits on? Though you possess
great riches, isn't someone in distress   160
unfairly? How do you explain the way
that ancient temples of the gods decay?
You bastard, why not make an allocation
from your hoard for your beloved nation?
(for surely business always comes out right   165
only for you!) O *someday* you'll invite
derisive laughter from your enemies!

When faced with doubtful choices, which of these
will come across as more self-confident?
A person who is snide and corpulent?   170
Or someone satisfied with simple things

who is afraid of what the future brings,
and, like a sage, in peace prepares for war.

So you may trust these words a little more,
since boyhood I have known Ofellus spent   175
huge assets to no greater an extent
than now in his more modest situation.
On farmland measured off for confiscation,
this tough tenant-farmer can be viewed
with sons and livestock claiming,

                         'I'd exclude   180
on workdays any more than smoked pig's feet
and vegetables, and if we were to meet
a long-lost visitor, or when it rained
a neighbor visited while we refrained
from working for a little while (a guest   185
who would be welcome), we would be impressed
not by the seafood city dwellers get,
but baby goat and chicken. Next we'd set
out for dessert some grapes that dangled down
and add split figs with nuts, then we would clown   190
around with drinking games where we obeyed
the edicts of depravity and prayed
to Ceres so that, like a stalk of grain,
she would arise—and she would ease the strain
on furrowed brows with wine.'

                        Let Fortune vent   195
her rage and manufacture discontent!
How much impoverishing can she do
with what she takes? Oh lads, how much have you
or I become diminished since the day
this new intruder picked this place to stay?   200
For Nature, with all of his real estate,
has never been inclined to allocate
one lot to me, himself or anyone.
He has already sent *us* on the run,
but *he* will be expelled by ignorance   205
of legal loopholes or malevolence

(or surely, as a last alternative,
by someone's heir who has more years to live).
Umbrenus stamped his name upon this field;
Ofellus did so once. It does not yield   210
to ownership, but use will pass from me
to others back and forth. Accordingly,
live bravely, and with your brave hearts withstand
the many challenges you have at hand.'"

~ Satire 3

DAMASIPPUS: "You're writing hardly anything at all
   so fewer than four times a year you call
   for parchment while unweaving what you've got
   and getting mad because an awful lot
   of wine and sleep aren't letting you produce   5
   a piece that's worth discussing. What's the use?
You fled the Saturnalia to be
   more sober for a while. All right, let's see
that promised work of art that must be praised!

Let's get on with it!
                You have *NOTHING!*

                                   Crazed,   10
you blame the pen. You pound your fist against
   the blameless wall, that stepchild of incensed
poets and gods. And yet. . .you had the look
   of someone marked for greatness if you took
a break and let yourself be welcomed by   15
   the warmth beneath your farmhouse roof. So why
pack Plato with Menander and skip town
   along with such companions of renown
as Eupolis and Archilochus? Were you
   serving envy by deserting virtue?   20
You will be vilified by everyone!
   You wretched piece of work, you have to shun
that slutty siren, Sloth—or else return
   contritely honors that you used to earn."

HORACE: "For offering this counsel, which is true,   25
    may gods and goddesses bestow on you
    a barber, Damasippus, but now tell
    me how you came to size me up so well."

DAMASIPPUS: "Since all my wealth was devastated by
    the Arch of Janus, making me rely   30
    upon my wits, I offer my advice
    on other people's business for a price.
    There was a period when I was keen
    to find a bronze that had been used to clean
    the feet of wily Sisyphus or sniff   35
    at what was poorly carved or too stiff
    when it was cast. As someone hard to fleece,
    I'd bid a hundred thousand for a piece.
    With deals for gardens or immense estates,
    I was without a peer, which illustrates   40
    why people on the street bestowed on me
    the nickname of 'the Man of Mercury.'"

HORACE: "I know, and I'm amazed this plague was purged,
    although it's stunning how disease emerged
    to take its place, as is the way when pain   45
    will migrate from an aching chest or brain
    into the gut or someone comatose
    becomes a boxer making bellicose
    responses nearly striking his physician.
    Assuming you're avoiding this condition,   50
    you are free to follow your own rules."

DAMASIPPUS: "O friend, don't kid yourself! As with most fools,
    you are insane—if you adopt the view
    the sales pitch of Stertinius is true.
    I copied down the things he had to say   55
    that so astonished me; on that same day
    he tried to comfort me and volunteered
    I should be nurturing a sage's beard
    and feeling happy that I had returned
    from the Fabrician bridge where I had yearned   60
    to jump into the river as my head

hung low—until, at my right side, he said,
'Don't take an action that you don't deserve!
False shame has plagued you, for you lack the nerve
to be regarded as a lunatic   65
among the lunatics, so first I'll stick
to asking what it means to be insane.
If found in you alone, I will refrain
from saying any more to interfere
with your attempt to bravely disappear.'   70

Chrysippus argues from his portico
(as does his flock) that those who do not know
their ignorance and blindly are compelled
by folly are insane. This rule is held
as true for all the masses, and applies   75
to mighty kings, though it exempts the wise.
Now learn why those who have been calling you
a lunatic are lacking judgment too.
As in the woods, where one mistake can force
a group to wander off its proper course   80
and then go back and forth (when someone takes
the right, another charges left), each makes
the same mistake, but in some different way
they all inevitably go astray.
To the extent you think you've lost your mind,   85
your duller critics drag their tails behind.
One kind of moron has unfounded fears,
so if an open stretch of land appears,
he moans about its rivers, cliffs and fires.
A different, denser sort of man aspires   90
to clear a path through flames and water, thus,
when cherished mother, noble sister—plus
father and multitudes of cousins—shout,

'There's a big ditch! There's a big cliff! Look out!'
he'll hear no better than Fufius heard   95
while drunk and slumbering through every word
of Iliona's speeches—even though
twelve hundred Catienuses were so
intently yelling, 'Mother, hear our plea!'

I'll show you that the mob's insanity ·   100
is just like everybody else's woes.
With ancient statues, Damasippus goes
insane. Is lending money in a deal
with Damasippus crazy? Let's get real!
Suppose this were the offer I conveyed: 105
'Here is a loan that need not be repaid.'

If you accept, are you of a sound mind?
Or are you weirder if you're not inclined
to grab loot from a willing Mercury?
You can record as my security   110
ten loans to Nerius.

                          Not satisfied?
Add deeds Cicuta botched! I can provide
much more—a hundred or a thousand bonds!
And yet some heinous Proteus absconds
despite these fetters! When he's dragged to court,   115
he laughs so strangely that his jaws contort,
and then he makes himself a boar, a bird,
a boulder—or a tree, if that's preferred.
If business matters that are badly planned
suggest you're mad, and, on the other hand,   120
shrewd business dealings mean that you are sane,
then trust me that Perellius' brain
is far more addled since he'll often say
he'll loan you cash you never will repay.

I am inviting you if you are pale   125
from self-promotion on a loathsome scale,
you lust for cash, dark tales, or luxuries,
or suffer from some spiritual disease;
come gather round and get your togas straight.

Approach me closer as I explicate   130
to each of you why you have lost your mind.
What must be given to the greedy kind
of person is some high-dose hellebore,
and maybe all of Anticyra's store
should be deservedly reserved as theirs.   135

Upon Staberius's tomb his heirs
were forced to chisel all of his bequests,
for otherwise they'd need to give the guests
a hundred pairs of gladiators—plus
a banquet supervised by Arrius   140
with all the corn that Africa could send.

'No matter if whatever I intend
is right or wrong, don't play my uncle's role!'
(within Staberius' prescient soul
was this, I think).

              What, then, was his intent   145
in settling on the requirement
that heirs engrave upon his stone the sum
of his estate? Throughout his life, he'd come
to label poverty a huge disgrace
and nothing riled him more, so that in case   150
by chance he died less wealthy by one cent,
he'd see himself as more incompetent:

'Indeed, all things—fame, honor, the divine
and human—give way to the bottom line
and its attractions! Someone who has grown   155
his stash of wealth will be just, wise, well-known
and brave, and king, and satisfy ambition.'

He had hoped for public recognition,
as if virtue made it come his way.
Did you observe a similar display   160
from the Greek Aristippus? He once told
his servants that they should discard his gold
in central Libya, since with their load
he thought their journey would be greatly slowed.
Which one is more insane? To substitute   165
new disagreement for an old dispute
is pointless. If a person went to buy
some lyres and, after buying, stacked them high
without concern for them or any Muse,
or bought some knives and lasts he couldn't use   170
because he's not a cobbler, or he paid

for sails although he is opposed to trade,
he would be accurately called insane
and blithering. And so what would explain
what differentiates him from a man   175
who hoards his gold and silver with no plan
about its use, and will not touch it, fearing
it like something he should be revering?
If someone with a club were lying low
to guard a giant pile of corn, and though   180
he owned it all, he wouldn't even dare
to touch one grain, and so instead would spare
himself expense by eating bitter greens;
if someone with a thousand jugs—that means
there's *nothing*—with *three hundred* thousand jugs   185
of Chian and Falernian still chugs
his rancid vinegar, or if, OK,
at nearly eighty he would sleep on hay
and leave pajamas rotting in a chest
(a feast for moths and grubs), he'd seem possessed,   190
of course, to only a minority
for most men suffer from this malady.
You god-forsaken geezer, why would one
protect this stuff? So that an heir—a son
or possibly a slave who has been freed—   195
can lap it up? Or do you dread real need?
Each day how badly would your coins be clipped,
I must inquire, if your salad dripped
with better oil? (your scalp too, which is gross
with unattended dandruff) Why, if close   200
to anything will keep you satisfied,
do you steal, lie and loot the countryside?
You're sane? If you had started throwing stones
at crowds, or slaves you purchased with no loans,
the boys and girls would call you quite insane.   205
There isn't any damage to your brain,
however, when you find your wife a noose
and kill your mother when you introduce
some poison in her food, and furthermore,
you are not doing this in Argos, nor,   210

like crazed Orestes, will your sword run through
and kill the woman who gave birth to you.
Or do you think he went mad once he killed
his parent, and no madness was instilled
by the fierce Furies right until the blade   215
he honed so well grew warmer as it stayed
within his mother's throat? But once they found
Orestes' mental state to be unsound,
there wasn't anything to castigate;
he dared not use his sword to violate   220
Electra, his own sister, or Pylades.
He taunted both of them with blasphemies;
she was a Fury, and he something vile
inspired by delusions brewed in bile.

Opimius, a pauper though he stored   225
away his gold and silver in a hoard,
used ladles from Campania to serve
the wine from Veii that he would reserve
for festivals, and drink the bitter wine
on other days. He started to decline   230
into a lethargy that was so great
his joyful heir began to celebrate
around his patron's strongbox with his keys.
His doctor, who was quick and aimed to please,
aroused him in this way: he had them haul   235
a table in, and then he dumped out all
his coins from sacks and had the household come
and make a full accounting of the sum.

This gets him sitting totally erect,
and then he adds this:

DOCTOR: 'If you don't protect   240
the things that you possess, a greedy heir
will expeditiously arrive to snare
it for himself!'

OPIMIUS: 'While I am still alive?'

DOCTOR: 'Just pay attention if you want to thrive!
Just *do* it!'

OPIMIUS: 'What do you advise I do?'   245

DOCTOR: 'Your meager veins will keep on failing you
   unless food bolsters your collapsing gut.
   You balk? Here, have some gruel.'

OPIMIUS: 'This rice cost *what?*'

DOCTOR: 'Eight cents.'

OPIMIUS: 'Alas, who cares if I am left
   destroyed by sickness, robbery or theft?'   250

DAMASIPPUS: "Who's sane then? He who's not a fool! The greedy?
   Madmen and fools!"

HORACE: "What?"

DAMASIPPUS: "If a man's not greedy,
   does it follow that he is insane?
   No, not at all."

HORACE: "Why, Stoic?"

DAMASIPPUS: "I'll explain:
   if I suppose Craterus takes the tack   255
   his patient's problem isn't cardiac,
   then is he well, and will he move around?
   No! He will say his illness is profound
   with symptoms in his kidneys and his chest.
   He's not a liar or a low-life pest;   260
   he gives the grateful Lares offerings
   of boar. He's brash and yearns for better things,
   so let him sail to Anticyra then!

   Indeed, what is the real distinction when
   you're hurling all you own into a pit   265
   compared to never utilizing it
   though it's available? It has been said
   that Servius Oppidius, who led
   a wealthy life by standards of his day,
   while nearing death decided to convey   270
   to his two sons their shares in land he owned
   outside Canusium. From bed he groaned,

'Once I had witnessed you, Aulus, hold
your nuts and knuckles in your toga's fold
while gambling and losing every toss,   275
and you, Tiberius, assessing loss
with great remorse and hiding dice in holes,
I feared that madness in two forms controls
the two of you, and you might track the fate
of Nomentanus while you emulate   280
Cicuta.
              Thus, I beg you in the name
of the Penates, see that *you* disclaim
more squandering, and *you* more acquisition,
since your father's taken the position
it's enough and Nature has defined   285
these limits. In addition, I will bind
you with an oath so fame won't stimulate
you two; if you become a magistrate
or praetor, you'll be damned and sent away!
Don't squander all your wealth with what you pay   290
for lupines, vetch and beans so you're bereft
of property and cash your father left
to you because you want to have a chance
to strike a pose for bronzes while you prance
and casually make your way, you nut,   295
around the Circus with a preening strut.
You're like the wily fox who imitated
the blunt lion, no doubt motivated
to win the praise Agrippa rates from us."

UNKNOWN SOLDIER: 'You gave the order, son of Atreus,   300
   that no one was to bury Ajax. Why?

AGAMEMNON: 'I am the king.'

UNKNOWN SOLDIER: 'I won't attempt to pry,
   since I'm a commoner.'

AGAMEMNON: 'Though evenhanded
   with regard to what I have commanded,
   if a man *believes* I am unjust,   305
   I let him speak to what he wants discussed.'

UNKNOWN SOLDIER: 'May the gods grant to you, most mighty king,
    a triumph over Troy so you can bring
    the fleet back home. Am I allowed to try
    a question and receive a prompt reply?'   310

AGAMEMNON: 'Your question?'

UNKNOWN SOLDIER: 'Why let Ajax, number two
    behind Achilles as a hero, who
    so often rescued the Achaeans, stink?
    Won't Priam and his tribe exult to think
    he is unburied, somebody by whom   315
    their children were denied a local tomb?'

AGAMEMNON: 'He's mad! While screeching, he inflicted death
    upon a thousand sheep, in the same breath
    he cried, 'The two of us together slew
    famed Menelaus and Achilles!'

UNKNOWN SOLDIER: '*You!*   320
    You who upon the Aulis altar placed
    your darling child, and not some calf, and laced
    her head with salt and grain, *you reprobate!*
    Did you believe you kept your thinking straight?
    Indeed, what has this crazy Ajax done?   325
    He wouldn't brutalize his wife and son
    when he unleashed his sword to kill the flock!
    Although he hurled obscenities to mock
    the tribe of Atreus, he never cut
    down Teucer—or Ulysses, even!'

AGAMEMNON: 'But   330
    in order to release the ships of war
    that were immobile on a hostile shore,
    it was appropriate that I appease
    the gods with blood.'

UNKNOWN SOLDIER: 'As everyone agrees,
    that blood is yours, you madman!'

AGAMEMNON: 'It is mine,   335
    though I'm no madman!'

DAMASIPPUS: "He whose thoughts align
   with thoughts that are opposed to what is true—
   so that it's hard to separate the two
   when mixed in with emotional distress—
   will be considered mad. It's more or less   340
   the same if anger or stupidity
   is what produces his futility.
   When Ajax kills some blameless lambs, he's mad.
   When for some empty honor to be had,
   you sin because it is 'appropriate,'   345
   is it still true your mental state is fit,
   and is your heart that's puffing up with pride
   undamaged by its evil? If one tried
   to hoist a glossy lamb upon a litter
   as if it were his daughter, had maids fit her   350
   in some gown, provided gold, and named
   her "Rufa" or "Pusilla" and proclaimed
   she should be married to a valiant man,
   a praetor would then promulgate a ban,
   and abrogate his legal rights, and give   355
   his custody to some sane relative.
   So is a person healthy in the head
   while sacrificing his own child instead
   of some unspeaking lamb?

Don't interrupt!

Thus, when stupidity becomes corrupt,   360
   it is the most extreme insanity.
   Somebody lacking in humanity
   will be a madman. When fame's glitz has trapped
   a person, he then will be thunderclapped
   by fierce Bellona, who delights in gore.   365

Now come with me so that we can abhor
   both Nomentanus and extravagance,
   for reason offers damning evidence
   that spendthrifts are insane as well as dumb.
   As soon as his inheritance had come   370
   in with a thousand talents, he decided

to decree that vendors who provided
fish, fruit, poultry or exotic scents—
or some of Tuscan Alley's godless gents—
and sausagemakers and the social whores,   375
and folks from the Velabrum or the stores
inside the covered market, should come back
next morning to his house. When a pack
of people came, a pimp had this to say:

'Whatever I or people here today   380
may have at home, believe me, it's for you!
Put orders in right now—tomorrow too!'

Now listen carefully to this reply
made by a juvenile but decent guy:

'Out in Lucania's deep snow you sleep   385
in boots so I can dine on boar; you sweep
the stormy seas for fish. I'm just not prone
to work that hard . . .
                    I don't deserve to own
so much! Just cart it all off! *You* can take
a million! *You* can do the same! *You'll* rake   390
in triple that, you with the wife who slips
so quickly from your house for midnight trips
when someone calls.'

                    Aesopus had a son
who—just to swill a million for some fun,
no doubt—unfastened from Metella's ear   395
a gorgeous pearl so it would disappear
in vinegar. Was he at all more sane
than if he tossed it in a sewer drain
or raging river? Famous brothers sired
by Quintus Arrius, those twins inspired   400
by vice, frivolity and decadence,
would dine on nightingales at great expense.
If somebody who has a beard enjoys
constructing little houses as his toys,
attaching tiny carts to teams of mice,   405
riding a wooden horse and tossing dice

for 'odd and even,' it would have to be
produced by mental instability.
If Reason proves it is more juvenile
to be in love than acting in this style,   410
and that it doesn't matter if you play
at building in the sand in the same way
you did when you were three, or you implore
and whimper, jarred by longing for your whore,
I ask you whether you would imitate   415
what Polemon did when he went straight?
Would you discard the signs of your malaise
(those elbowpads, cravats and small bouquets),
just as he did when, on a drinking spree
(or so they say), he surreptitiously   420
slipped garlands from his neck once he had heard
his fasting master's first rebuking word?
Go offer apples to a pouting brat
and they will be rejected just like that!

'*Pleeeeease* take them, Poochie.'

                              '*NO!*' is his response.   425

If you *don't* offer, they are all he wants.

How is a lover who has been thrown out
much different when he can't decide about
returning to his former destination,
yet he leaves without an invitation   430
and hangs around the doorstep that he hates?

'When of her own volition she awaits
my presence, even now should I not go?
Or should I think of ending all my woe?
Should I return? *Not even if she pleads!*'   435

Behold the servant, who by far exceeds
this lover when it comes to being wise:

'O master, things which do not utilize
measure and common sense thwart common sense
and rationally fashioned arguments.   440
When you're in love, there are these evils: war,

and peace exactly as it was before.
If someone took on these affairs that shift
around much like the restless winds that drift
in random ways, and were to persevere   445
toward finding certainties, he wouldn't clear
things up much more than if he were to seek
to go insane through logic and technique.'

What? With Picenum's apples, when you spit
the seeds out and rejoice each time they hit   450
the vaulted ceiling, are you in control?
What? When you let that childish babble roll
off your worn palate, can you still maintain
that you should be regarded as more sane
than one who builds toy houses as his field?   455

Add blood to this stupidity and wield
the sword to stir the flames! I say to you:
since Marius killed Hellas and then threw
himself off a great height, was he possessed?
Or will the charge he's mentally distressed   460
be something you excuse at the same time
that you condemn that person of a crime
through games with words, as is so often done.
There was an aging freedman who would run
at dawn through shrines and crossings, though he'd stay   465
away from food, and with clean hands he'd pray,

'Just me!'
        then add,
                'Is that so hard to do?
Protect *just me* from death! For gods like you,
it's easy!'

           All his ears and eyes worked well,   470
although an owner, if he planned to sell,
would never grant a warrant for his mind
(unless he wanted lawsuits). For this kind
of person too, Chrysippus would assign
them to Menenius' fertile line.

'You, Jupiter, who send and end great pain,'   475
proclaims a mother whose sick son has lain
in bed five months, 'if quartan fevers spare
my boy, then on the morning you declare
that everybody must abstain from food,
I'll have him standing in the Tiber nude!'   480

If some fortuity or his physician
saves him from this dangerous condition,
his crazy mother will still kill him, thanks
to leaving him on icy river banks
so fever can return. What evil prods   485
her mind to think this way? Fear of the gods?
The eighth-ranked sage Stertinius, a friend,
provided me with these weapons to defend
myself from smears made with impunity.
If someone charges me with lunacy,   490
then he will hear from me the same attack
and come to see what dangles down his back
unnoticed."

HORACE: "Stoic, since you hope to make
a profit after what you had to take
in losses selling everything you had,   495
which stupid actions make *you* think *I'm* mad
(for there's not just one type, and it does seem
to me I'm sane)?"

DAMASIPPUS: "What? Does Agave deem
herself a person lacking self-command
exactly when she's holding in her hand   500
the severed head of her unlucky child?"

HORACE: "I'll cede to truth, and I am reconciled
to my stupidity—and madness too.
Expound on this a little: in your view,
which of my faults is so debilitating?"   505

DAMASIPPUS: "Listen, you're building first-class—imitating
the big shots, in other words, although
you're only two feet long from head to toe—

and yet when Turbo has that air, you scoff
as he parades in armor falling off   510
his body. Are you less ridiculous?
Or is it right that you're meticulous
in mimicking whatever that you see
Maecenas do, and yet you couldn't be
less similar and you can't take him on   515
because you're puny.
                     When a frog had gone,
a calf's hoof crushed her children, all except
the one who told his mother he'd been stepped
upon, and all his siblings murdered by,
a beast of huge proportions. In reply,   520
she asked, 'Was it *this big?*' as she inflated.

'Half as big again!' he indicated.

'Would you say it was *this big* instead?'

As she inflated more and more, he said,
'You could explode and never be the same!'   525

This image nearly fits you; fan the flame
with all your verse! If someone writes while sane,
you are the one who does it in that vein.
Your awful temper has to be ignored . . ."

HORACE: "Enough!"

DAMASIPPUS: "A lifestyle that you can't afford!"   530

HORACE: "You, Damasippus, must retain some poise!"

DAMASIPPUS: "Infatuation with a thousand boys,
  a thousand girls!"

HORACE: "O greater lunatic,
  I ask that you excuse one not as sick!"

∽ Satire 4

HORACE: Where *were* you, Catius, and you're off *where*?"

CATIUS: "I'm out of time! I'm eager to prepare
    some notes about a new analysis—
    a kind that will surpass Pythagoras
    and what's-his-name whom Antyus subdued   5
    and learned Plato!"

HORACE: "I admit it's rude
    to interrupt so inconveniently,
    but, friend, I'm asking you to pardon me.
    If something is escaping from you now,
    I'm sure you will retrieve it anyhow.   10
    It's knack or knowledge; be that as it may,
    you are extraordinary either way!"

CATIUS: "Indeed, that was my worry—how to keep
    it in my mind because it was so deep
    and handled deeply!"

HORACE: "Can you speak his name?   15
    A Roman citizen or one who came
    from somewhere else?"

CATIUS: "I will recite for you
    his rules, but outing him I just can't do!

    The more extended eggs—keep *those* in mind
    because their flavor is far more refined,   20
    and they are whiter, firmer, and contain
    male yolks. A cabbage grown with little rain

is sweeter-tasting than suburban yields,
and nothing's worse than stuff from soggy fields.
Suppose a friend of yours appears one night.   25
Since stringy chicken blunts the appetite,
while it's alive it's wise to drown it in
unprocessed grape juice that's Falernian,
which makes it tender. Mushrooms are the best
when picked in meadows—*never* touch the rest!   30
Black mulberries, when plucked before the sun
gets fierce, provide health benefits to one
who eats them after lunching. A mistake
Aufidius would regularly make
was drinking strong Falernian diluted   35
with some honey. Empty veins are suited
only for mild vintages; it's best
at first if weaker stuff can cleanse your chest.
And if your bowels are moving hard and slow,
mussels or common shellfish always blow   40
the blockage out, and baby sorrel's fine
as well—though *only* served with Coan wine!
New moons will make the common shellfish swell,
but harvests from some oceans won't excel.
The purple Baiae cockle can't compete   45
at all with giant Lucrines. Oyster-meat—
Circeian; urchins—from Misenum's coast.
Luxurious Tarentum loves to boast
about its gaping scallops. Don't profess
to know the art of dining well unless   50
you've fully mastered all these rules of taste:
fish scooped from fancy counters are a waste
if you don't grasp which sauce will be the best,
and which, if grilled, will drop a drowsy guest
back on his elbow; if a man abhors   55
lackluster meat, let acorn-fattened boars
from Umbria depress his rounded dishes,
for Laurentian is not delicious—
having only sedge and reeds for food;
some vineyard venison just can't be chewed;   60

a gourmet hunts the haunches of a hare
in heat; for fish and fowl, I'm not aware
of prior palates whose opinion gauges
their proper qualities and proper ages.

Some people's skills produce a pastry puff;   65
regardless, it will never be enough
to focus on one thing, like one who yearns
for wine that isn't bad with no concerns
about the oil for seafood. If you try
some Massic wine beneath a cloudless sky,   70
its coarseness mellows in the air of night
and scents that jar the nerves will lose their bite,
but straining it with linen is a way
to hurt it; it will lack the same bouquet.

An expert mixes Sorrentine with dregs   75
of his Falernian, then uses eggs
of pigeons to collect the sediment
with care because, when making its descent,
the yolk attaches to the residues.
As drinkers start collapsing, what renews   80
their vigor is grilled shrimp and escargot
from Africa—without the lettuce, though,
for after wine it floats without digesting
in acidic guts (which keep suggesting
sausages and ham as remedies).   85
Indeed, hot slop from squalid stands would please
them even more!
               It is your obligation
that you master basic preparation
of a compound sauce. A heavy wine
with some sweet olive oil, combined with brine   90
so foul you would imagine it had come
from reeking barrels of Byzantium,
provides your base. Boil. Spice. With a light hand,
sprinkle Corycian saffron. Let it stand,
then top it off with just a bit of juice   95
from what Venafran olive trees produce

with their pressed berries.
                      Tibur apples fare
less well in taste whenever you compare
Picenum's, though they are more beautiful
in their appearance. Grapes most suitable   100
for potting are Venunculan; to dry
them, Albans are the best. You'll see that *I*
was first to place these raisins in a curve
around the apples. *I* was first to serve
a blend of lees and paste of pickled fishes,   105
and first to use two dainty, spotless dishes
when one sifts white pepper and black salt.
It is a horribly barbaric fault
to spend three thousand in the marketplace,
then squeeze a sprawling fish into the space   110
a tiny platter can provide. It makes
weak stomachs queasy if a servant takes
a goblet in his hands when they are slick
from snatching samples with a secret lick,
or if an ancient bowl has built up scum.   115
Plain napkins, brooms and sawdust—why become
so cheap? Such things are shameful to ignore!
Imagine sweeping your mosaic floor
with palm-leaf brooms still filthy with debris
or draping Tyrian upholstery   120
with dirty valences! Though they are cheap
and easy to provide, if you don't keep
remembering these things, it's more than fair
to criticize you for your lack of care—
unlike those items typically ignored   125
which only wealthy tables can afford."

HORACE: "Wise Catius, I plead with you by all
    the gods and by our friendship to recall—
    no matter where you go—you must invite
    me to this presentation, for, in spite   130
    of your repeating it so faithfully,
    you as the translator can't offer me
    as much enjoyment; add his look and face,

which luckily for you is commonplace,
though cheapened by the things you've seen transpire.   135
In any case, I have this strange desire
to travel to the fountains in the distance
and guzzle rules for rapturous existence."

~ Satire 5

ULYSSES: "Tiresias, I want more information!
  This question needs a fuller explanation:
  what kind of merchandise and strategy
  would make me whole again financially?
  . . . Why do you laugh?"

TIRESIAS: "For you, most shrewd of men,   5
  why isn't it enough to sail again
  to Ithaca, and then to cast your eyes
  upon your house?"

ULYSSES: "O you who tell no lies,
  why can't you see? I've come back home stripped clean
  of cash and assets, as you had foreseen,   10
  and hordes of opportunists did not spare
  the herds and storage cellars I had there.
  What's more, without some cash a noble birth
  and virtue do not match what seaweed's worth!"

TIRESIAS: "To be blunt, since it's poverty you dread,   15
  discover new techniques to get ahead!
  Suppose you have a thrush or some such thing;
  you should release it, letting it take wing
  until it finds a glittering estate
  that's owned by someone old. Let the Lar wait   20
  so he can taste; send fruit and products raised
  upon your tidy farm and have him praised
  above the Lar. Though he has always lied,
  lacked breeding, stained his hands with fratricide,

and slipped his chains, when walking you should go   25
  along the outside if he wants it so.

ULYSSES: "What! Cover up some dirty Dama's flank?
  At Troy, against the men of highest rank,
  that's not how I behaved."

TIRESIAS: "Then you'll be poor."

ULYSSES: "I'll make my steadfast soul endure this chore;   30
  I've done worse.
                  Fortune-teller that you are,
  enlighten me right now about how far
  I need to go to rake in cash and wealth."

TIRESIAS: I've *told* you, and I tell you now: use stealth
  while trawling for the wills of older men   35
  in every place that you can find, and then
  if one or more have nibbled on the bait
  but slipped away, don't brood or hesitate
  to hone your craft despite your consternation.
  Whenever there is Forum litigation   40
  (whether minor or significant),
  become a lawyer for the litigant
  who's rich and childless, though a jerk—the sort
  who hauls a better person into court
  without a bit of shame or legal basis.   45
  Shun the citizen with stronger cases
  or a pedigree if there's a son
  or fertile wife at home. Tell anyone
  called 'Publius' or 'Quintus' (first names please
  their precious ears):

                  'Your moral qualities   50
  have made us allies. I have learned that laws
  are two-edged swords; I can defend a cause
  of action. I would rather let my eyes
  be plucked out than for you to realize
  a loss on trinkets or be vilified.'   55

Send him back home to tend his tender hide,
  and then you will become his advocate!

Persist relentlessly and never quit
regardless if 'the scarlet Dogstar splits
the silent statues' or, if stuffed with bits   60
of rich tripe, Furius 'is spewing drops
of spit on snowy Alpine mountaintops.'
Someone will nudge another, then complain,

'Why can't you see how he has suffered pain,
provided help to friends, and been astute?"   65

More tuna will be swimming down this route,
and ponds will bulge. What's more, if someone wealthy
has a son, acknowledged but unhealthy,
you should, in order not to be betrayed
by obvious attention you have paid   70
to someone single, cozy up with care
and hope that you are named the backup heir,
then if some tragic fluke should take the son
to Orcus, it will leave you as the one
to fill the void.

                These gambits should succeed.   75

If given his last testament to read,
be sure that you refuse and push away
the tablets as you subtly survey
arrangements covered in the second line
of Page One. Quickly see if there's some sign   80
that you're sole heir or with a multitude.
Often the minor bureaucrat rebrewed
to be a magistrate deceives the crow
whose beak has split as far as it can go,
and Nasica, who hunts a legacy,   85
will give Coranus grounds for levity."

ULYSSES: "Are you insane? Or is it that you tease
    me by revealing doubtful prophecies?"

TIRESIAS: "O scion of Laertes, all these things
    that I describe are what the future brings,   90
    or not, for great Apollo gives to me
    the gift of seeing what will come to be."

ULYSSES: "But, nonetheless, provide me, if you're able,
   with interpretation of your fable."

TIRESIAS: "The moment will arrive when a young man,   95
   despised by Parthians, born of the clan
   of eminent Aeneas, will command
   respect from everyone on sea and land,
   while Nasica's tall daughter (she who dreads
   to *satisfy* her obligations), weds   100
   the brave Coranus. After this event,
   the son-in-law has something to present:
   he tries to give the father of his bride
   his will and have it read, though he's denied
   a while by Nasica, who in the end   105
   reads silently and comes to comprehend
   that neither he nor relatives received
   bequests—except a reason to be peeved!

   I'll add this point to that: if some old guy
   who's lost his mind can be 'persuaded' by   110
   a shrew and freedman, treat them as your team!
   Praise them so they will speak of their esteem
   for you when you're away!
                  This helps as well:
   it's best that *you* assault the citadel.
   Suppose this idiot is writing verse   115
   that couldn't possibly be any worse,
   I'd praise it! Does he like his one-night stands?
   Beware if he must tell you his demands!
   Make sure the better person in the deal
   will get Penelope."

ULYSSES: "*What?* You don't feel   120
   concerned that she could be seduced, *do you?*
   she who has been so virtuous and pure,
   whom all those suitors never led astray?"

TIRESIAS: "I do! The youngsters who would come her way
   were chintzy, zealous for her recipes,   125
   not Venus—which explains Penelope's
   devotion. But if she just tastes a bit

of geezer-generated benefit
from entering a partnership with you,
just like some bitch with greasy hides to chew,   130
she won't be scared away. Let me unfold
a tale that happened back when I was old:
An ancient nasty hag at Thebes was hauled
away for burial like this: as called
for in her will, a semi-naked heir conveyed   135
her well-oiled body so she could evade
his clutches through the last resort of dying.
I think her motive was he kept on trying
to be grabby while she was alive.

Tread carefully. Don't shirk or overstrive.   140
A bigmouth ticks off those who snarl and frown;
say only 'yes' and 'no.' Keep ducking down
like Davus in the comedy; appear
as if you've totally succumbed to fear.
Approach obsequiously. If winds rise,   145
some covering is what you should advise
for his beloved head. What you must do
in crowded areas is plow right through
with shoulders low so he escapes the throng.
Lend him an ear though he has talked too long.   150
Does he delight in being overpraised?
Until he says, "*Enough!*" with both hands raised
up to the heavens, you should press the matter
and inflate the windbag with your chatter.

When he has freed you from long servitude,   155
and worry, and you know with certitude
it's not a dream, you'll hear, 'A quarter-share
is given to Ulysses as the heir!'
Say, 'Now my buddy Dama has departed!
Who could be as loyal and stouthearted?'   160
If you're somewhat able, shed a tear
to hide your joy. Don't make the tomb austere
if you select it; let your neighbors praise
the classiness the funeral displays.
If there's an older co-heir who keeps hacking,   165

Assure him if a farm or house is lacking
in his share, you would be serious
about deep discounts.
                         Now imperious
Proserpine is dragging me to Hell!
Have a good life, and I must say farewell!"   170

ᵔ Satire 6

These were the things I hoped my prayers would bring:
some land, a kitchen garden and a spring
that's always flowing by a house below
a modest stand of trees. The gods bestow
on me far more and better; I'm content.   5
Except to make these blessings permanent,
O son of Maia, I won't try to gain
by asking more of you. If I refrain
from adding assets by malevolence
or causing losses through my negligence   10
and waste; if I don't offer prayers like these:

"O let me own abutting properties
intruding into mine; for they distort
the borders of my farm!"

       "O let some sort
of lucky break provide me with a pot   15
of silver, like that guy who, when he got
his treasure, bought and plowed the very land
on which he labored as a hired hand,
and so became enriched by being tied
to Hercules."

    If I am satisfied,   20
and grateful for my personal possessions,
I beseech you for these intercessions:
fatten up my flocks and the domain
that I am master of—except my brain—

and, as you have invariably been,   25
remain my most important guardian.

So when I've left the city life to stay
secure within my mountain hideaway,
how should I first illuminate my views
through satire with my heavy-footed Muse?   30
My vain ambitions haven't brought me low,
and neither have the southern winds that blow
oppressively as autumn's bleakness offers
vicious Libitina fuller coffers.

Father of dawn or, as you would prefer   35
to be called, "Ianus," for whom people stir
while starting labors, as the gods decree,
when I begin this lyric, sing with me!
In Rome you send me off to testify
about some friend:

                    "*Move!* Others could reply   40
before you! Keep on pushing!"

                                One must go
although across the land the north winds blow
or winter drags the snowy days in arcs
of smaller size. My plain and clear remarks
may haunt me someday when I feel the crush   45
of people in the street and have to brush
aside the slow.

                "What do you mean by *that*,
you madman?" and "What are you driving at?"

(a dirtbag curses me and vents his wrath)

"Must everything be shoved out of your path   50
if you're returning to Maecenas filled
with memories of him?"

                        For sure, I'm thrilled,
and it's like honey, but when I return
to the grim Esquiline, the people churn

around me with their hundreds of requests   55
for business guidance:

         "Roscius suggests
tomorrow you should meet him at the Well
before the second hour."

         "Personnel
at Treasury request you not forget,
Quintus, to come back for a meeting set   60
for later in this day about some new,
important business critical to you
and others."

        "Have Maecenas certify
this stack of forms!"

           If you respond, "I'll try!"
he adds, "With *work* you can!" and will not bend.   65

The seventh year—almost the eighth—will end
before long if it's measured from the date
Maecenas started to assimilate
me in his group—like someone you would take
along while on a carriage ride to make   70
some chit-chat such as:

        "Is this sundial right?"

"So, is the Thracian Chicken a fair fight
for Syrus?"

        "These new morning frosts will freeze
you if you let them!"

        and the pleasantries
we safely drop into a leaky ear.   75
Through every day and hour of the year,
he feels more jealousy from everyone.
The people call him "Fortune's favored son"
for joining "him" at games or Campus play.
A chilling bit of gossip makes its way   80

from Rostra to the streets; if I'm around,
the passers-by will ask me to expound.

"Dear fellow, you must know! What have you heard?
You hang with gods—you must have gotten word
about the Dacians!"

                    "I have nothing. No."   85

"You're such a joker!"

                         "If it is not so,
the gods may strike me dumb!"

                              "What? Will there be
land grants in Italy or Sicily
when Caesar gives the veterans their due?"

When I assert my ignorance, it's true   90
they marvel at the only mortal man
who holds his tongue as often as he can.
These kinds of useless things consume my days,
which aren't devoid of prayers:

                         "When will I gaze
at you, O country house, and can devour   95
the books of ancient authors, waste an hour,
and sleep so I, oblivious to strife
connected with an ordinary life,
can ponder?"

                    "O when will they serve the beans
(Pythagoras' relatives) and greens   100
with bacon grease in adequate supply?"

O nights and feasts of gods! My friends and I
would feed ourselves before my Lar and make
a gift to them from what we ate, then take
the rest to shameless servants. With insane   105
restrictions loosened, any guest could drain
a cup of any strength as he saw fit
so any one of them could guzzle it
unwatered, while a wimp could marinate

more sweetly, which thus would provoke debate—   110
though not about some mansion or retreat
or whether Lepos lacks a dancer's feet—
but things of more significant concern
and which are detrimental not to learn:

Does wealth or virtue give men satisfaction?   115

What leads to friendship—calculated action
or correct acts?

                    And what will reveal
the nature of the good and its ideal?

While all of these events are happening,
my neighbor Cervius keeps chattering   120
about how it relates to old wives' tales.
Accordingly, if anybody hails
Arellius' wealth and doesn't say
a word about his stress, he starts this way:

"There was a country mouse some time ago,   125
or so the story's told, who thought he'd show
a city mouse around his humble den
since guest and host were friends from way back when.
Though crude and focused on his stash of food,
he would adopt a looser attitude   130
for entertainment. Why say any more?
He wasn't grudging with his chickpea store
or the long oats, or half-chewed bacon strips
and his one raisin carried in his lips,
because he hoped that choice would override   135
his friend's contemptuous displays of pride,
for his reluctant teeth would hardly deign
to touch them while the lord of this domain
napped on fresh straw, and snacked on emmer wheat
and darnel while rejecting every treat.   140
The city dweller asked him in the end,
'How do you get a benefit, my friend,
by living life in such a sorry state
on a steep, wooded hill? Why did you rate

the savage woods as somewhere you preferred   145
to people and the city? Trust my word,
since mortal souls are given out to all
who live on earth, and neither big nor small
can flee from death, let's hit the road as friends!
Do not forget, fine fellow, how life ends   150
so quickly; live a happy life that's blessed
with many joyful things!'
                          These words impressed
the hick; he took the leap of leaving home
without much thought so that the pair could roam
as they had planned until the time was right   155
for them to creep through city walls by night.
Once night had reached the zenith of its trip
across the skies, by paw this pair would slip
inside a fancy house, one that displayed
that gleaming scarlet cloth on couches made   160
of ivory with baskets piled up high
containing many foods uneaten by
those at the blow-out feast of yesterday.
Then, once the country mouse was squared away
and stretching out upon a purple cover,   165
in his waiter's garb the host would hover
and provide more food while doing things
in slave-like style, first licking what he brings
out to be served. The other mouse, at ease,
delighted in his opportunities,   170
and in good spirits played the happy guest—
then crashing doors abruptly dispossessed
them from the couches! Terrified, they flew
around the dining room, and terror grew
as the great mansion echoed with the sounds   175
of baying coming from Molossian hounds.

And so the country mouse made this reply:

'I do not need this life!' then said, 'Goodbye!
Safe in my den from covert agitation,
simple vetch remains my consolation.'"   180

~ Satire 7

Davus: "I've listened now for quite a while, and crave
   a word with you, but I'm a fearful slave."

Horace: "Davus?"

Davus: "Yes, Davus, master's faithful friend
   and chattel—one you reckon, in the end,
   is good enough to live."

Horace: "Come, exercise   5
   December's freedom, for it satisfies
   our ancestors' intentions! Have your say!"

Davus: "Some men rejoice in vice and never sway.
   More waver; righteousness is where they head,
   then they embrace perversity instead.   10
   Infamous for three rings he used to wear,
   Priscus would sometimes leave his left hand bare.
   He lived as one of those impulsive types,
   and every hour he would change his stripes.
   From his immense estates this fellow ran   15
   to low-life haunts no self-respecting man
   could leave without experiencing shame.
   A playboy while in Rome, he then became
   an Athens sage (born, surely, during visions
   of Vertumnus changing his decisions).   20
   A bum named Volanerius, with gout
   he earned that left him crippled all throughout
   his fingers, paid a guy to throw his dice
   into the box. When focused on one vice,

 you are less sad and on a better track   25
  than fighting with a rope that's taut, then slack."

HORACE: "You punk! Can you explain—*sometime today*—
 just where this crap will lead?"

DAVUS: "To you, I'd say."

HORACE: "How so, scumbag?"

DAVUS: "For men of old you praise
 both their prosperity and civil ways,   30
 but if some god could suddenly transport
 you there, you'd stubbornly attempt to thwart
 him, since you either cannot justify
 what you are saying or aren't standing by
 what's right with any guts, for you're still stuck 35
 and cannot pull your foot out from the muck.
 At Rome you hunger for the countryside,
 and yet while in the country you provide
 long tributes to a city far away.
 What fickleness! And if there were a day   40
 nobody had invited you to dine,
 you'd *claim* your simple salad was just fine,
 and, like one forced to party, praise the news
 and hug yourself for missing out on booze!
 Suppose Maecenas makes a late request   45
 and summons you to be his dinner guest
 just when the time for lighting lamps is near.
 'Get *moving* with some oil! Can't *someone* hear?'
 is what you bitch and moan before you flee.
 Your entourage and Mulvius break free,   50
 while simultaneously cursing you
 in terms I can't repeat. 'Yes, it is true,'
 Mulvius says, 'I am subservient
 to my own gut. When sniffing nourishment,
 I lift my snout. I'm weak, an imbecile;   55
 what's more, I hang out where they're serving swill.
 Since you're the same as me—inferior,
 perhaps—why run me down as if you were

a man of better morals, though you hide
your viciousness with words you've prettified?'   60

What happens when you are revealed to be
a fool of worse stupidity than me—
who cost five hundred drachmas? Do not try
to terrify me with your evil eye;
restrain your fist and bile as I explain   65
the information I could ascertain
from what the doorman of Crispinus taught:
another person's wife is how *you're* caught;
for Davus it's a whore. Since we've both failed,
which one of us should be the one who's nailed   70
upon a cross? When nature's urges prime
me for some sex, whoever at the time
lies naked in the lantern-light, and takes
the pounding of my swollen tail, and makes
me be her stallion while she wildly mounts   75
me from the top until her buttocks bounce,
will do. She then declares I've had my turn,
with my good name intact and no concern
about the same equipment being used
by bigger names. But you, when you refused   80
to wear the signs of status—a knight's ring
and Roman dress—you went out partying
not as a citizen of high repute
but as a *Dama*, someone dissolute,
and with a perfumed face obscured from view.   85
Isn't your cover now the same as you?
Frightened, you slink inside her house, then quake
as fear and passion battle. Does it make
a difference if you're auctioned off for cash
so that you will be battered with a lash   90
and run through with a sword or if you squeeze
yourself inside some nasty box with knees
and head together at the instigation
of the maid, who knows each violation
of her wayward mistress? Aren't there ways   95
a husband married to a wife who strays

can ask for justice to control the pair?
For plaintiffs, isn't this result more fair
since she, at least, won't change her rank or clothes,
or take the top position in the throes   100
of her illicit passion? Since this wife
is scared of you, and wouldn't bet her life
on you, her darling lover, would you dare
to put yourself into the stocks and share
your good name, body, life and whole estate   105
although your mistress is consumed with hate?

You have escaped.

                    You'd think you'd be concerned
and careful after everything you've learned,
and yet you ask about more avenues
of terror and destruction you could choose.   110
O chronic slave, what type of brute absconds
and then returns perversely to his bonds?
'I am not an adulterer,' you say.
By Hercules, because I wisely stay
away from silver, I am not a thief!   115
Remove the possibility of grief,
then ease the bridle, and before too long
our nature is revealed as it goes wrong.
Are you *my* master, when *you're* subjugated
by so many highly celebrated   120
people and events, and though you're freed
three times, and even four, you don't succeed
in shedding your sad insecurities?
On top of points I've made, I'm adding these,
which are no less important: whether he   125
who is slave-managed is a "deputy"
(which is the way you people classify)
or a "co-slave"—for you, which one am I?
Despite the bossy way that you behave,
you're surely just another sorry slave   130
performing like a puppet on a string.

Then *who* is free?

                        One who is wise and brings
restraint to all he does, who doesn't fear
poverty, chains or death, who will adhere
with zeal to principle despite desire   135
and scorns awards to which he could aspire,
who is himself a polished, rounded whole
too smooth for anybody to control,
and who can fend off Fortune's lame attacks.

Do *you* possess these traits?

                              Some woman lacks   140
five talents so she hounds you, makes you sore,
refuses to allow you past her door,
and drenches you with icy water. . .*then*
insists on your returning once again.
Don't leave your neck inside this yoke of shame!   145
'I'm free! I'm free!' is what you must proclaim—
so do it!
                    You'll do nothing of the kind!
Indeed, a brutal master rides your mind
relentlessly—when you are weary, jabbing
you with sharpened spurs as well as grabbing   150
on your reins if you attempt to balk.
For instance, raving lunatic, when you gawk
at paintings by Pausias, tell me why
I'm more offensive when I'm dazzled by
some ochre-chalk or charcoal artistry   155
depicting, even down to straining knee,
Rutuba, Fulvius, and Pacideianus
so it feels like war has come upon us
as they slash and dodge while brandishing
their weapons so it seems like the real thing.   160
While Davus is a 'rogue' and 'parasite,'
you are 'an expert' and 'an erudite
authority on every fine antique,'
I'm nothing if I'm led astray and sneak
a taste of fresh-baked pastry.
                              Do your soul   165
and lofty sense of virtue lose control

at fancy meals? The stomach's tyranny
is more pernicious when it comes to me.

Why?

      Sure, my back's been whipped, but when you chase
gourmet delights—at no small cost—you face   170
no less a punishment for, after all,
an endless banquet leaves a taste like gall,
and feet that now regret they took the bait
refuse to bear the wicked body's weight.
Or is it preferable to indict   175
this action: under cover of the night,
a servant trades a body-brush he stole
for grapes? But isn't it a servile role
if someone feels compelled to sell off land
to stuff his gut? Moreover, you can't stand   180
to be alone one hour, you don't give
free time its due, and, like a fugitive
or stray, you flee your life and ease your pain
with wine, and then with sleep. It's all in vain
considering that your companion, gloom,   185
is closing in, and as you run will loom
behind you."

HORACE: "Can you find a rock for me?"

DAVUS: "And why is that?"

HORACE: "Where might my arrows be?"

DAVUS: "There's verse or madness coming from this man!"

HORACE: "Get out of here as quickly as you can—   190
or at my Sabine Farm I'll reassign
you to the job of 'Fieldhand Number Nine.'"

$\backsim$ Satire 8

HORACE: "How did you like the dinner hosted by
 that rich Nasidienus? I did try
 to have you come to dinner yesterday,
 but was informed you'd been well on your way
 toward getting very drunk since noon."

FUNDANIUS: "No meal   5
 was ever better."

HORACE: "If it's no big deal,
 describe which course first tamed your growling gut."

FUNDANIUS: "Boar brought in from Lucania was what
 we started with—one captured, said the host,
 in gentle Austral winds. Around the roast   10
 were tangy appetizers such as these:
 young turnips, radishes, greens, Coan lees,
 fish-pickle, parsnips—items that excite
 an overstimulated appetite.
 Once all the appetizers had been cleared,   15
 a slave with tunic hiked up high appeared
 and rubbed the maple table carefully
 with purple woolen rags while stray debris
 of the variety that tends to cloy
 for guests was cleaned up by another boy.   20
 Then, bearing the Caecuban wine supply,
 swarthy Hydaspes came sashaying by—
 almost as if he were some Attic maiden
 clutching Ceres' talismans—while laden

down with undiluted Chian wine   25
was Alcon. Next the host would use this line:

'If Alban or Falernian would please
you more, Maecenas, we can serve you these.'"

HORACE: "The *miseries* of wealth! But I'm intent
to know, Fundanius, of those who went   30
to dine, who was your big celebrity?"

FUNDANIUS: "They sat me at the top, and next to me
Viscus of Thurii, then Servilius
Balatro with, I think, Vibidius
(each shadowing Maecenas like a ghost)   35
and Nomentanus was above the host.
Below them there was Porcius, who'd clown
around with everyone by scarfing down
a pastry in one gulp. The one who took
on showing us what we might overlook   40
was Nomentanus.
                    For the others, they—
I mean to say 'we rookies'—put away
the shellfish, fowl, and fish, which tasted more
bizarre than any food we'd had before,
as we would suddenly become aware   45
once he had offered us such novel fare
as sole and turbot organs. Next he said
that what had made the honey-apples red
was picking them beneath a crescent moon
(why this would matter, I would just as soon   50
you heard from him. . .)

                    Vibidius then cried
out to Balatro, 'We will both have died
in vain if we don't drink until he's broke,'
and called for larger cups, which would provoke
some paleness in 'the keeper of the food,'   55
who had no fear of greater magnitude
than dread of thirsty drunks, since they malign
a person recklessly and heat their wine

so that it dulls a palate's subtleties.
Balatro and Vibidius would seize   60
whole jugs of wine then turn them over so
their mugs from Allifae would overflow.
The other guests soon followed, all except
for those upon the lowest couch, who kept
their tankards free of damage. What was laid   65
out next for us was moray eel arrayed
upon a plate entirely surrounded
by shrimp swimming. Then the host expounded,

'This was caught while pregnant, since the meat
degrades as soon as spawning is complete.   70
The sauce's recipe was: oil (first-pressed)
from the Venafran cellar that's the best;
fermented Spanish fishgut sauce; a wine
that's five years old and nurtured on a vine
from native shores—but only with some heat   75
(when warmed up, Chian wine just can't be beat!);
white pepper, vinegar that comes from spoiling
of Methymnean grapes. I taught the boiling
of green rocket with sharp elecampane
in sauce before those others. In that vein,   80
Curtillus used unwashed sea-urchin juice
because brine fails to match what shells produce.'

Just then, the canopy upon the wall
came crashing down, which made more dirt fall
than what is stirred by northern winds that blow   85
through farmland of Campania. Although
we feared a worse result, once we discerned
there was no risk of harm, our poise returned.
With his head drooping badly, Rufus cried
as if his adolescent son had died.   90
Where, in the end, would all of this have led
if wiseguy Nomentanus hadn't said
these words to cheer his friends?
                                        'Which god's more cruel,
Fortune, than you? You really like to fool
with human business!'

                    Varius pursued   96
attempts to choke down laughter as he chewed
his napkin. While he held his nose aloft
to everybody there, Balatro scoffed,
'These are constraints of living, so your fame
won't match your efforts to promote your name.   100
Are you in agony and feeling dread
from every kind of worry—that your bread
might burn, your sauce might need a little zest,
and all your slaves might not be coiffed and dressed
appropriately? Add calamities   105
as well like these collapsing canopies
or when a person's lackey slips and breaks
a serving-dish. However, failure makes
it clear when generals or hosts possess
great genius, which is hidden by success.'   110

Nasidienus then replied this way:
'May all the benefits for which you pray
be granted by the gods for you've impressed
me as a decent man and gracious guest!'
and asked for slippers. Then you would have seen   115
small groups with secrets whispering between
themselves on every sofa so there was,
before much longer, something of a buzz."

HORACE: "There are no shows I'd rather see. So, after
that took place, what was the cause of laughter?"   120

FUNDANIUS: "Just as Vibidius had cracked a joke
by asking if the flagon also broke
(because they had no tankards to supply)
and we were feigning laughter, spurred on by
Balatro, you, Nasidienus, came   125
back, but appearing not the same,
as if improved techniques might change your fate.
Then servants entered with a massive plate
displaying legs and wings of a male crane
seasoned with just a touch of salt and grain;
with liver from a goose, fig-fed and white;   130

and hare—with just the limbs—as if a bite
of leg without the loin would taste the best,
and then we saw some roasted blackbird breast
and wood-dove with the backside taken out—   135
sweet things unless the host opines about
their traits and places they originated.
Once we had properly retaliated
by refusing any of his food,
we fled as though Canidia had spewed   140
her venom—worse than that of snakes you find
in Africa—on those we left behind."

Notes

❧ Book I

Satire 1

l.1 Horace's patron, Maecenas (70–8 B.C.), was one of the towering figures of Horace's time. He was born wealthy and continued to expand his wealth as he became a member of Octavian's inner circle. He was a statesman given to compromise and moderation, an extraordinarily generous patron of the arts, and an inept poet. His enthusiasm for games and recreation was often seen by more traditional Romans as childish or effeminate.

Maecenas' star did decline later in his career. Most accounts for his fall from favor blame his wife, Terentia, but the details of those accounts vary. For thoughtful discussions of *amicitia* (the relationship between a patron and those he sponsored) in Roman society, see generally Schlegel at 52–56; Bowditch, *Horace and the Gift Economy of Patronage* (Berkeley: University of California Press, 2001).

These first three satires are usually called the "diatribe" satires. But see Freudenberg at 7. Although Horace makes a few innovations and "protests too much" about his differences from Lucilius, these three satires would have felt familiar to Roman audiences who had read or heard Lucilius. For an overview of scholarship about the etymology of the term *satura* ("satire"), see Schlegel at 147, n.2; Coffey at 11–23.

l.16 According to the scholiasts, Fabius was a Stoic philosopher. See Brown at 91, n.14. For Horace, he represents prolixity.

l.76 The Aufidus is the modern-day and more tame Ofanto River. It runs through Campania, Basilicata, and Apulia into the Adriatic Sea near Barletta.

l.87 An early commentator attributed the reference to "that Athens miser" to the misanthropic Timon of Athens. See Brown at 95, nn. 64–67.

l.91 In Greek mythology Tantalus was the son of Zeus and the nymph Plouto as well as an ancestor of the ill-fated House of Atreus. As a bribe to forgive his theft of ambrosia and disclosure of secrets of the gods, he offered up his son, Pelops, as a sacrifice by cutting him up, boiling him, and serving him as food. As punishment, Tantalus stands in the underworld in a pool of water beneath a tree with the proverbial low-hanging fruit. When he reaches for fruit, the branches raise it out of reach. When he bends down for water, the pool recedes. From this myth we get the word "tantalize."

l.127 Ummidius is unknown.

l.136 Naevius is unknown. He might have been a Lucilian character, see Brown at 98, nn. 101–2, or a poet, perhaps a satirist, of a previous generation, see Coffey at 22. For Nomentanus, see note to Satire II.1, ll 33–34.

ll.155–158 Freudenberg documents the stock nature of this simile. See Freudenberg at 42–43.

ll.160–161 This line echoes Book III of Lucretius' *De Rerum Natura*. See Schlegel at 24.

Satire 2

l.5 Hermogenes Tigellius was a famous singer and, apparently, a heartthrob whom Horace found annoying.

l.20 Fufidius may have been a moneylender described by Cicero. See Brown at 102, n. 12.

l.25 Boys exchanged a purple-edged toga for a white one at the age of fifteen or sixteen, see Brown at 102, nn. 16–17, a fairly standard age across cultures at which teenagers tend to get themselves into trouble.

l.29 Although the plays of Terence tend not to resonate with modern audiences, he was revered in his era. The reference here is to the father in Terence's *Heauton timorumenos* ("The Self-Torturer").

l.35 Maltinus is unknown. The scholiasts' view that this is a veiled reference to Maecenas seems highly unlikely given both Maecenas' generosity to Horace and his capacity to punish the disloyal.

ll.38–39 Rufillus and Gargonius are unknown. Apparently we should be grateful for their obscurity.

l.43 Marcus Porcius Cato (234–149 B.C.), commonly known as Cato the Elder, was a farmer, soldier, and statesman known for bravery, rectitude, and pious sayings reflecting traditional Roman values.

l.49 Cupiennius is unknown. Given the play on the Latin word *cupire* ("to lust"), it is probable that he is a fictional character.

l.61 Galba is unknown.

l.64 Gaius Sallustius Crispus (86–34 B.C.), generally referred to as "Sallust," was a controversial politician closely tied to Julius Caesar. The censor Appius Claudius Pulcher removed him from the Senate in 50 B.C. for sexual misconduct. He was reinstated in 49 B.C. and in 46 B.C. served as praetor. As a reward for military services, Caesar appointed him governor of Nova Africa, where he distinguished himself with unusually oppressive and corrupt conduct. He went on to write several histories that are generally admired but are sometimes criticized for bias toward Julius Caesar.

Although in his heyday Sallust was a powerful figure, one should recall that his influence had declined in his later years and that he died around the time that Horace probably wrote this satire. Sallust was known for an affectation of trying to imitate the pithy rectitude of Cato the Elder, so it is likely that Horace had his tongue safely in his cheek when he portrayed Sallust as an example of a moral man.

ll.75–76 An *ancilla togata* ("white-robed miss") was a prostitute. Marsaeus and Origo are unknown.

ll.88–94 This incident seems to be drawn from reports by Cicero. Fausta, daughter of the dictator Sulla, was born in 86 B.C. and married Milo, but she was notoriously unfaithful. According to Cicero, Villius was an acquaintance of Milo's. Longarenus is unknown. See Brown 109 at nn. 64–67.

l.109 Cerinthus is unknown.

ll.126–127 Lynceus, the mythical son of Aphareus and Arene, was an Argonaut who killed Castor. He was so famed for his eyesight that he was believed to be able to see things in the ground. Hypsaea is unknown.

l.129 These exclamations are a parody of an erotic epigram of Philodemus. See Brown at 110, nn. 92–93. See also l. 171 below.

l.134 Catia is unknown.

l.142 Brown aptly describes silk from the Greek island of Kos as "famous, if not infamous, for its diaphanous quality." See Brown at 111, nn. 101–2.

ll.147–149 Brown points out that this lyric is probably a condensation of an epigram by Callimachus. See Brown at 111, nn. 105–10.

l.171 Philodemus of Gadara (?110–?38 B.C.) was an Epicurean philosopher and poet who studied with Zeno of Sidon before moving to Rome where he became a teacher of Virgil.

ll.178–179 In Roman mythology Ilia was the mother of Romulus and Egeria was a nymph with a gift of prophecy. See Brown at 113, nn. 125–27.

l.192 Fabius is the gasbag Stoic discussed above at I.1, l. 18.

Satire 3

l.4 This Hermogenes Tigellius is probably the same popular singer mentioned at I.2, l. 5, although this point has become a matter of academic dispute. See Rudd (1966) at 292, n. 15.

l.5 This reference is the only mention of Octavian in Book I of the *Satires*. He would not take the title of "Augustus" until 27 B.C., a few years after Horace finished the *Satires*. See Brown at 115, nn.4–7. He is also mentioned at II.1, l. 28.

l.9 Bacchus was the god of wine and "Io Bacche" was a drinking song.

l.17 Juno was the sister/wife of Jupiter and the mother of many deities.

l.22 Salt was a highly valued part of the Roman diet.

l.26 One million sesterces was a lot of money—exactly the amount of property required to qualify as a senator.

ll.35–36 Novius is unknown. It is possible he is a type based on *novus* ("new") as in our "nouveau riche." Maenius is possibly a figure borrowed from Lucilius. See Brown at 116, n.21.

ll.38–40 I have tried, badly, to imitate the wordplay of *ignoras, ignotum,* and *ignosco* in the original with know, notice, and no. The wordplay in the original is a bit strained too.

l.46 Aesculapius, the god of healing, had a temple at Epidaurus where snakes were used as part of the healing rituals. See Brown at 117, nn.25–27.

l.66 Balbinus was probably a victim of the proscriptions, which were seizures of the property of political enemies. Hagna's name suggests she was a Greek freedwoman. See Brown at 118, n. 40.

ll.72–78 As jarring as these lines may be for modern readers, Horace's attitude probably reflects the most enlightened thinking of his time by suggesting that people should treat a disabled person well and with kind humor. In his era people with disabilities were generally not so fortunate, and frequently suffered ridicule and abuse on top of their physical pains. Horace himself suffered from chronic eye inflammation, as you will see in Book I, Satire 5.

l.111 This line contains Horace's first hint of self-deprecation, a vein of humor he will mine more deeply in Book II.

l.128 Crucifixion was a punishment generally reserved for slaves.

l.130. Labeo is unknown.

l.137 Ruso is unknown. The Kalends were a time for debt repayment. See Brown at 122, nn. 87–88.

l.143 Evander was a legendary Arcadian king who migrated to Italy and assisted Aeneas. See Brown at 122, n. 91.

l.196 Chrysippus was a Stoic philosopher.

l.200 Though some scholars differ, in my opinion the reference is to Hermogenes Tigellius, the popular singer.

l.203 Alfenus is sometimes thought to be a reference to a lawyer and supporter of Octavian named P. Alfenus Varus, but that might be a stretch. See Brown at 126, n. 130.

l.215. Freudenberg suggests that Crispinus is an anagram for Chrysippus, the Stoic philosopher. See Freudenberg at 40.

Satire 4

ll.1–3 Old Comedy is said to have arisen from the revelry of Dionysian celebrations at the time of the establishment of Greek democracy in the year 510 B.C.. Of the three great writers of Old Comedy mentioned by Horace, only the works of Aristophanes survive to any great extent. Practitioners of Old Comedy had great artistic freedom, and their ability to mock the people and institutions of their time made their work immensely popular. Freudenberg argues that Horace's history of Old Comedy is deliberately ham-handed. See Freudenberg at 17–18.

Cratinus (?520–?423 B.C.) had a long and successful career and may have won his last competition in his nineties for his lost play *Wineflask*. According to contemporary accounts, he wrote twenty-one comedies.

Eupolis (?446–411 B.C.) originally was on good terms with Aristophanes, but their relationship deteriorated due to mutual charges of plagiarism. Alcibiades was one of Eupolis' targets, and there are reports that Eupolis was killed by Alcibiades, but it is more likely that Eupolis died in battle. Only fragments of his seventeen known plays survive.

Aristophanes (?446–?388 B.C.) is one of the major figures of Western literature. Eleven of his forty plays survive, including *The Clouds*, *The Birds*, and *Lysistrata*, in which women withhold sex from their husbands until they end the Peloponnesian War.

ll.8–9 This line has subtle undertones. While Horace is praising Lucilius by linking him with the giants of the past, he is also arguing that Lucilius' work is highly derivative and by implication that his own work is more creative. It helps set the stage for the full onslaught that begins in line 13.

l.11 The "keen-nosed" reference is a complex one suggesting both astuteness and snobbery.

l.21 See note at I.3, l. 215.

l.32 Fannius is unknown, but Horace elsewhere describes him as an associate of the crooner Tigellius. See Brown at 129, nn.21–22.

l.43 Albius is unknown. It is possible that Horace was playing on "album" (white) as a trope for innocence and gullibility, although that conjecture is a bit of a stretch.

l.50 Farmers tied hay to the horns of dangerous oxen to mark them as dangerous. See Brown at 130, nn. 34–35. Exactly how the farmers tied the hay to such animals is an interesting point to ponder.

l.55 Public ovens and water troughs were provided to the poor in Horace's time. See Brown at 130, n. 37.

l.58 As Horace starts speaking in the first person singular, you should be cautious about distinguishing between the historical Horace and the character he is creating. See Schlegel at 11–14.

l.68 Horace is probably referring to Cicero. See Brown at 131, nn.45–46.

ll.73–78 This plot was so common in Greek and Latin comedy that this passage does not clearly refer to a particular play.

ll.79–80 It may be that the subtleties of this reference make it difficult to grasp Horace's point fully here, but these lines do feel like a non sequitur even if you read the Latin as introducing a counterexample. Although scholars disagree about these lines with some vehemence, the reference here may be to Titus Pomponius Atticus (109–32 B.C.), a Roman patron of the arts who as a young man preserved his inheritance during a period of civil unrest by moving it and himself to Athens.

ll 89–90 This quotation is from Ennius and refers to the temple of Janus, where the doors were kept open during wartime. See Brown at 132, nn. 60–61.

l.97 Sulcius and Caprius are unknown.

l.103 Birrius and Caelius are unknown.

l.106 The allusion to the pillar is not completely clear, but it is probable that booksellers would set up stands around large columns in busy public places.

ll.107–108 Hermogenes Tigellius was the crooner who got on Horace's nerves. See note on I.2, l. 5 above.

ll.134–135 I have tried here to replicate the wordplay around "Liber" and "liberque" (here "liberties"). Liber was the equivalent of Bacchus, the god of wine and revelation.

ll.140–141 Rufillus and Gargonius are unknown.

ll.143–144 Petillius Capitolinus was a well-known violator of the public trust, although the exact specifics of his misdeed remains debated today. See Brown at 135, nn. 93–95.

l.163 Baius is unknown.

l.167 Scetanus is unknown.

l.170 Trebonius is unknown.

ll.213–214 The Romans viewed Jews as proselytizers. Jews were also seen as exotic due to their practice of circumcision and their dietary constraints. Although the Jewish community in Horace's time was quite impoverished, it was fairly large, and Octavian treated Jewish residents of Rome reasonably benevolently given the standards of the time. Flavius Josephus reported a lawsuit in which eight thousand Jews joined. Since women and children could not litigate, scholars have estimated that Rome's Jewish population was probably between thirty and fifty thousand. See generally Harry J. Leon and Carolyn Osick, *The Jews of Ancient Rome* (1960; Peabody, Mass.: Hendrickson, 1995); Joan Goodnick Westenholz, *The Jewish Presence in Ancient Rome* (Jerusalem: Bible Lands Museum, 1994).

Satire 5

l.1 In this satire Horace leaves Rome as a hanger-on on a diplomatic mission to negotiate a reconciliation between Octavian and Antony. The mission did happen, although scholars savage each other debating whether it was a mission that occurred in the autumn of 38 B.C. or a similar mission in the spring of 37. See Freudenberg at 56–57. Despite external reports confirming that these missions actually took place, some scholars have used similarities between Satire 5 and a travel poem of Lucilius called *iter Siculum* to argue that Satire 5 is entirely or almost entirely fictional. Since Lucilius' poem exists only in fragments, commentators have been free to assume that the lost pieces of his poem would prove that Horace's piece is even more derivative than they can prove with the available texts.

This view is a triumph of erudition over common sense. While Horace undoubtedly recognized at some point that life was imitating art and then played up that angle in the poem, the verified details and the authentic feel of the poem's many peculiar details strongly suggests that what Horace recounts took place at least to some extent—and there is no good reason to assume otherwise. Did he let truth get in the way of a good story? Undoubtedly not.

This satire is similar in spirit to Horace's mock epics, such as Book I, Satire 7 and the parody of Homer in Book II, Satire 5. Horace's audience probably knew about his role in this diplomatic trip, but he erases any doubt by reminding us in line 47 that their purpose was to "help embittered friends to compromise." He then in the following line deflates that grand purpose with the mundane report that "I smeared black ointment on my swollen eyes."

This almost Seinfeldian insistence on focusing on the petty aspects of life instead of the big picture is part of the humor and the point of this poem. Part of Horace's call to moderation is a reminder to us all that the intoxicating power of myth regularly drives man to cruelty; perhaps nowhere is this call more clear than in his uncharacteristically coarse description of men's origin in Book I, Satire 3. In Book II, Satire 3, Horace's stubborn refusal to submit to a glorious retelling of an important moment of Roman history is an oblique way of telling us to stay focused on those things in our own lives that we can control and to make decisions about those things with moderation and decency.

l.3 Horace started in Rome and went in a fairly straight line to the site of Brundisium at the "heel" of the "boot" of Italy. They took the Appian Way until they reached Beneventum.

l.5 It is probably correct that Heliodorus is a pseudonym for Apollodorus, a renowned scholar whose name would not fit within Horace's meter. See Tenney Frank, *Classical Philology* 15 (1920): 393. But see Emily Gowers, "Horace *Satires* 1.5: An Inconsequential Journey," *Proceedings of the Cambridge Philological Society* 39 (1993): 48–66 (suggesting an obscure writer of travel poems).

l.7 Forum Appi ("Appius' Market") was a small town twenty-seven miles past Aricia at the site of modern Foro Appio. It was named after Appius Claudius Caecus (a populist consul who was the Robert Moses of his time); he began work on the Appian Way in 312 B.C. See Brown at 140, n. 3.

l.8 A sixteen-mile canal through the treacherous Pomptine marshes ended at Forum Appi. See Brown at 140, n. 4.

l.12 The Appian Way is one of the marvels of Roman engineering. It used innovative techniques, such as lime cement, to create an unusually level road through difficult terrain from Rome to Brundisium (modern Brundisi). In addition to improving commerce and quality of life, the Appian Way allowed Rome to consolidate military and political control over southern Italy, much like the railroads of nineteenth-century America.

l.13 The water was probably "vile" due to the proximity of the Pomptine marshes.

ll.15–19 Here again Horace rises to a mock-epic tone then immediately deflates that move with a return to the mundane.

l.39 Feronia was a pre-Roman Italian goddess equated with Juno.

l.45 L. Cocceius Nerva was consul in 39 B.C.. See Brown at 142, nn. 27–29.

l.51 Fonteius Capito, a friend of Antony's, accompanied Maecenas on the 37 B.C. mission mentioned above at l. 1. He was later chosen as consul in 33 B.C.

l.52 The legendary Marcus Antonius (?89–30 B.C.) (generally known in English as "Mark Antony") was a charismatic, if erratic, politician and warrior. Despite a notoriously wild youth that hardly suggested a great future, he settled disagreements with Julius Caesar and became perhaps his most important supporter. After narrowly missing warning Caesar about the assassination attempt that killed him, he fled Rome dressed as a slave and then formed a triumvirate with Octavian and Marcus Aemilius Lepidus. The collapse of this triumvirate in 33 B.C. led to a vicious civil war in 31 B.C. which ended when Octavian defeated Antony at Actium and Alexandria. Antony committed suicide with his lover, Queen Cleopatra VII of Egypt, in 30 B.C.

l.54 Fundi is a town now known as Fondi about twelve miles past Anxur. See Brown at 143, nn. 34–36.

l.55 Aufidius Luscus is almost certainly a fiction—Aufidius may allude to the raging but murky Aufidus River Horace mentions at I.I 76, and the secondary meaning of *luscus* is "obscure" or "unintelligible." Schlegel rests on the primary meaning of "blindness" to suggest a touch of self-parody based on Horace's own eye issues and both figures' work as a *scriba* (which means both writer and bureaucrat). Her view is probably a stretch. See Schlegel at 67.

l.60 The most famous member of the Mamurrae was Julius Caesar's notoriously commercially and personally corrupt chief engineer. See Brown at 144, n. 37.

l.61 Aulus Terentius Varro Murena was the brother by adoption of Maecenas' controversial wife Terentia. He became consul in 23 B.C. but was executed in 22 B.C. for conspiring against Augustus. See Brown at 144, n.38.

l.65 Publius Vergilius Maro (70–19 B.C.), commonly known as Virgil, is of course the author of the *Aeneid* and one of the greatest poets of all time. At the time of this trip, however, he had not yet fully established his genius. He probably had completed the *Eclogues*, may have started the *Georgics*, and probably had not started the *Aeneid*.

Lucius Varius Rufus (74–14 B.C.) was a poet and a friend of Virgil. Varius and Virgil introduced Horace to Maecenas. Horace considered him a great epic poet, but only fragments of his work survive.

M. Plotius Tucca was a poet about whom we know little except that he and Varius were Virgil's literary executors. They refused to honor Virgil's dying wish that his incomplete *Aeneid* be burned, and Augustus later ordered the executors to complete the masterpiece.

ll.86–87 Sarmentus and Cicirrus are unknown, although there has been some speculation about their identities. Skinny Sarmentus ("sarmentum" is Latin for "stick") may have been a slave freed by Maecenas, which raises the possibility that some of the humor of this piece may be more of the "inside" variety. See Brown at 145, nn. 51–54.

l.90 The Oscans were a southern Italian tribe centered in Campania.

l.119 Vulcan was the god of fire.

l.124 Apulia (modern Puglia) is a region of southeastern Italy.

l.126 Atabulus was the local personification of the scorching Austral (southern) winds. See Brown at 148, nn.77–78.

l.146 In Greek legend Diomede was one of the great warriors in the assault on Troy, and was even said to have wounded Aphrodite and Ares.

l.160 Romans believed that Jews were highly superstitious. Brown notes at 149, nn.99–100 that the name "Apella" was probably wordplay on circumcision (*a* means "without" and *pellis* means "skin").

Satire 6

l.1 Lydia was a kingdom in western Turkey famous for its wealth. Herodotus claimed that the Lydians were the first to mint coins and the legendarily greedy king Croesus was a Lydian. Herodotus also claimed that large numbers of Lydians emigrated to Etruria, where they became known as Etruscans. Etruscan lineage had great snob value in Rome, somewhat akin to having come to America on the *Mayflower*.

l.2 See note on I.I, l. 1 above for a discussion of Maecenas.

l.13 Servius Tullius was supposedly sixth in succession from Romulus and reigned from 578 B.C. until he was murdered in 535 B.C. by Lucius Tarquinius. According to Roman legend, he was also the son of a slavewoman and Vulcan, the god of fire. Despite some humble lineage, Romans revered Tullius for his benevolence and successful public works projects.

Laevinus is possibly a failed minor politician named P. Valerius Laevinus, but this identification is uncertain. See Brown at 153, nn.12–14.

l.15 Valerius is the P. Valerius Publicola who led the expulsion of the Tarquins in 509 B.C.

l.16 Lucius Tarquinius Superbus (also known as "Tarquin the Proud") reigned from 534 to 510 B.C. He hacked a bloody path to the throne by murdering his wife, brother, and father-in-law (the Tullius discussed above at l. 13).

l.27 While losing a battle with the Latins, a consul named Publius Decius Mus (?–340 B.C.) reportedly gained victory for the Romans through a "devotio," an elaborate ritual asking the gods of the Underworld for victory in battle in exchange for death in battle.

l.28 Appius Claudius Pulcher was a notoriously strict censor who served in 50 B.C.

l.34 Although I could not resist "proletariat" as a rhyme for "chariot," the Marxist tinge of "proletariat" is not totally inapt given Horace's focus on class distinctions in this satire.

l.36 Tillius is unknown.

ll.41–42 These straps and stripes were emblems of senatorial rank.

l.45 Barrus is unknown. A "barrus" was an elephant, but there is no apparent play on words here unless one reaches to call the elephant and the subject of this passage exotic animals.

ll.56–57 Dama, Dionysius, and Syrus were stock names for slaves.

l.59 The Cadmus of mythology founded Thebes with the slaying of a dragon. By sowing the dragon's teeth, Cadmus harvested a crop of armed men whom he encouraged to fight until only five survived. These five became the ancestors of Theban nobility. We should probably assume that the inspiration for nicknaming an executioner "Cadmus" was the mythological character's penchant for gory violence.

l.60 Novius is almost surely a type—a *novus homo* ("new man")—and not a historical individual. A *novus homo* was a term used to describe the first man in a family to obtain a curule magistracy, which included censors, consuls, praetors, and two curule aediles. A holder of one of these titles was allowed to use the *sella curulis* ("chair of state") as a symbol of authority.

l.62 Paullus Aemilius Lepidus and Valerius Messalla Corvinus were among the few aristocrats supporting Octavian at this time. See Brown at 155, nn. 41–42.

ll.67–68 The rime riche in the translation is not laziness; the phrase "libertino patre natum" is repeated at the end of lines 45 and 46 of the original text. Horace may have overstated his father's humble status; some scholars speculate that he may have been a well-heeled member of the Sabine aristocracy who briefly suffered enslavement as a punishment for some offense. See Williams, "*Libertino Patre Natus*: True or False?" in S. J. Harrison, ed., *Homage to Horace: A Bimillenary Celebration* (Oxford: Clarendon Press, 1995), 296-313.

l.87 *Satureiano* ("Saturean") is the Greek (hence more elevated in this context) adjective for items from the area of the affluent town of Tarentum mentioned in Book II, Satire 4 as the home of the finest oysters. Freudenberg suggests that the term is a swipe at Lucilius, a wealthy man who would inspect his properties in this region by horseback. See Freudenberg at 60–61.

l.90 Perhaps "nine months" is a liberty with history taken to suggest rebirth. Perhaps not.

l.159 See l. 87 above.

l.182 Marsyas was a satyr who challenged Apollo to a musical contest where the winner could do what he wished with the loser. This reckless bet, predictably, turned out badly for Marsyas because Apollo tied him to a tree and flayed him alive. Brown suggests, almost surely correctly, that Horace is referring to statue of Marsyas in the Forum where Romans gathered for business discussions. See Brown at 163, nn. 119–20.

l.183 See l. 60 above.

l.188 Natta is unknown.

l.191 The Campus Martius ("Field of Mars") was an open area for recreation.

Satire 7

l.1 This satire is so widely regarded as Horace's worst that there have been reports that a scholar or two damaged their academic careers by attempting to defend its literary value. Blessedly, it is the briefest of his satires.

Why do we find this satire dull and did Horace's contemporaries feel similarly? The spectacle of people rushing into court is not as reflexively funny for us as it apparently was for Romans, and it is also hard for us to relate to the nuances of the political puns that end this satire. Moreover, in other satires Horace's brief mock heroic bits (frequently immediately deflated) never extend as long as they do here, and one can have too much of a good thing. While Romans may have chuckled at a few passages that leave modern readers cold, it is probably safe to assume that this satire was not a huge hit with Horace's readers either.

ll.1–7 Persius is unknown. In 43 B.C. Rupilius was a praetor who was proscribed by the triumvirate at the instigation of Octavian, and then fled to join Brutus in the province of Asia. Cicero refers to a Rupilius as a tax collector in Bithynia. See Brown at 155–56, n. 1. If Rupilius did become a tax collector, it may explain the origin of this satire's litigation, since Clazomenae (modern day Kliziman in Turkey) was in the province of Asia and Clazomenae enjoyed immunity from taxes under Roman rule. Brutus' suicide in 42 B.C. makes the timing of this interpretation possible but a bit dicey.

Rupilius may well have been living at the time of this satire, but would have been an exceedingly safe target for criticisms of greed and overreaching given his history with Octavian.

l.5 Barbershops were places for gossip. Scholars since at least Fairclough have been quick to associate the "red eyes" of line 5 with Horace's chronic eye inflammation, but it is unlikely that Roman barbershops were crowded with people with pink eye or similar conditions. I have always felt that for Romans, as for us, red eyes must have been associated with nocturnal revelry, and in my opinion that is the better interpretation even though most scholars disagree.

l.13 Barrus and Sisenna are unknown, and it is not clear whether this Barrus is the same Barrus of Book I, Satire 6. See note on I.6, l. 45 above.

ll.14–30 As tangled as the syntax of this passage is in my translation, it is worse in the original; I may have done readers a disservice by smoothing it out a bit. The point of the technique perhaps is that the narrator is so caught up with the excitement of the story that his words come out in a tumbling torrent.

ll.23–24 For information on Diomede, see note on I.5, l. 146 above. In the *Iliad*, when Diomede declined to fight the less imposing Glaucus, Glaucus exchanged his golden armor for Diomede's bronze armor.

l.27 Bacchius and Bithus were gladiators.

l.29 Marcus Junius Brutus (85–42 B.C.) was the famous senator who had a leading role in the assassination of Julius Caesar.

l.36 The Dogstar was Sirius, a bad omen whose rise in late July was associated with drought and pestilence. See Brown at 168, nn. 24–25.

l.41 Praeneste, the modern Palestrina, is twenty miles east of Rome. See Brown at 168, n. 28.

ll.47–50 Although not crystal clear, the text at ll. 33–34 suggests that Brutus is in the audience, which would explain a direct address to Brutus. The Latin puns on *rex* ("king"). Unable to duplicate that specific pun, I have punned on throat slitting and ruthless self-promotion with the word "ahead." See generally Schlegel at 159, n. 14 for a discussion of critical response to the original pun.

Schlegel makes an interesting defense of this satire's widely derided conclusion. In my opinion, though, she misreads the politics of the time by suggesting that Horace displayed "gleeful daring in allowing Persius to implicate Brutus. . .", at 88, since under Octavian it required about the amount of daring to knock Brutus that it took for a Democrat to knock Richard Nixon in 1975. However, she is probably right that the closing pun is "a strategy and makes the verbal exchange and its sudden finish precisely equivalent to the finish of physical combat" (ibid.). One might extend her point and note Horace's general fondness for the abrupt ending with the unexpected twist, a commonplace of mime plays. While others might read deeper meanings into this tendency, for me it reminds me of the entertainment function of classical poetry that is now, sadly, largely absent in contemporary poetry.

Satire 8

ll.1–4 Alexander has observed that the opening of Collodi's *Le avventure di Pinocchio* strongly echoes the opening of this satire, except that the phallus becomes a nose. See Alexander at 346–47, n.1. Figs were associated with fertility and the inexpensiveness of figwood made it attractive for routine uses.

ll.4–11 Priapus was a fertility god generally portrayed with a giant phallus. As in this satire, Romans used statues of Priapus the way American farmers use scarecrows to ward off birds. These figures spawned an odd genre of poetry, collected in the *Priapeia*, consisting of epigrams attached to Priapean statues which threatened human trespassers with violence, including particularly painful anal penetration. While authorship of these oddities is uncertain, many scholars believe that some of the finest poets of Horace's generation contributed to this collection. Schlegel at 91 notes parallels between the opening of this satire and the *Priapeia*. See generally Richard Hooper, *The Priapus Poems: Erotic Epigrams from Ancient Rome* (Urbana: University of Illinois Press, 1999)

l.11 The Esquiline is the largest of the Seven Hills of Rome. In Horace's time it was a splendid neighborhood that had been built over a dump and a squalid burial ground for paupers. One of the gardens on the cleaned-up hill was named for Maecenas.

ll.17–18 Nomentanus and Pantolabus are unknown.

l.34 Despite considerable effort and speculation by scholars, Canidia is unknown. See generally Daniel Ogden, *Magic, Witchcraft and Ghosts in the Greek and Roman Worlds: A Sourcebook* (Cambridge: Oxford University Press, 2002).

l.37 Sagana is unknown.

l.46 Hecate was the goddess of sorcery and "Queen of Ghosts." A figure imported from Asia who did not fit easily in the Greek pantheon, she was worshipped at crossroads. The usual sacrifice to her was a dog.

l.47 Tisiphone was one of the Furies.

ll.53–55 Julius, Pedatia, and Voranus are unknown.

l.62 Schlegel notes at 97–98 possible wordplay on *testis* (here "one who saw it all") and "testicle."

Satire 9

l.1 The Sacred Way was the route connecting the Palatine and the Forum where Rome's most sacred shrines were located. See Brown at 176, nn. 1–2

l.16 Bolanus is unknown.

l.27 The Tiber is the major river that flows through the city of Rome.

l.35 Varius and Viscus are fellow poets.

l.37 Hermogenes Tigellius is the crooner discussed at I.2, l. 5 above.

l.53 Vesta was the goddess of home, hearth, and family.

l.93 Aristius Fuscus was a friend of Horace. There is some evidence that he wrote comedies.

ll.107–108 The Romans thought that the Jewish practice of circumcision was exceedingly strange and that Jews were highly superstitious due to their many dietary and other rituals.

l.117 The plaintiff in Roman litigation touched a witness on the ear if the witness consented to serve—a symbolic way of charging the witness to remember his duties. See Brown at 182, nn. 76–77.

l.120 Apollo, among his many other duties, was the god of poetry and, therefore, a natural protector of Horace. He was also a favorite of Octavian. Mazurek correctly points out that Horace's salvation is at best marginal, and that he would still be accompanied by the bore once he agreed to testify by allowing his ear to be touched. See Tadeusz Mazurek, "Self-Parody and the Law in Horace's Satire 1.9," *Classical Journal* 93 (1997): 1–17. However, Mazurek's argument that "Apollo" here is actually a reference to the mischievous Fuscus instead of an actual *deus ex machina* is an overreading.

Satire 10

l.1 I have excluded eight lines that appear at the beginning of this poem in some later manuscripts because the scholarly consensus is that they are spurious. But see Hendrickson, *Classical Philology* 11 (1916): 249–69; 12 (1917): 77–92.

l.3 The pun on walking and meter is in the original.

l.9 Decius Laberius (?105–43 B.C.) was a knight (*eques*) who forfeited his rank by being one of the two first prominent figures to write Roman mimes. Do not think of slim, silent, annoying white-faced men when you think of a Roman mime play. Think instead of riotous low comedies with occasional tinges of oblique political commentary. In 46 B.C. Caesar ordered Laberius and his chief rival to produce mimes in which they themselves appeared. Laberius' prologue, which survives and was translated by Ben Jonson, cheekily complains about how disrespectful it is to impose such a task on a man of sixty. Caesar awarded the prize to Pubilius Syrus, but restored Laberius to the rank of knight.

l.24 For a discussion of Old Comedy, see I.4, ll. 1–3.

l.26 Hermogenes Tigellius is the heartthrob crooner so disliked by Horace.

l.29 Calvus was a poet who was similar in temperament to and a friend of Catullus—even though Catullus referred to him as *salaputium disertum* ("eloquent dwarf"). Little of his work survives.

Gaius Valerius Catullus (?84–54 B.C.) was the leading figure of a group of poets known as the "neoterics" and is widely admired for his wit, creativity, and passion.

l.30 The importation of Greek and other foreign words into Latin was both common and commonly criticized. Similar arguments about the purity of the French language take place today in France.

l.34 For debate about the identity of Pitholeon of Rhodes, see Susan Treggiari, "Pompeius' Freedman Biographer Again," *Classical Review* n.s. 19, 3 (December 1969): 264–66.

l.36 Falernian and Chian were fine wines.

l.39 Petillius is perhaps one of the tribunes investigated by the Senate for embezzlement in 187 B.C. See Tenney Frank, "Some Political Allusions in Plautus' *Trinummus*," *American Journal of Philology* 53, 2 (1932): 152.

l.41 M. Valerius Messala was a famous soldier, statesman, orator, and literary patron of the arts whose circle included Tibullus and Ovid. Like Horace, Messala fought for Brutus and Cassius at Philippi, but at Actium was on Octavian's side. The scholiasts suggest that a Gellius Publicola was Messala's brother and that Pedius was somehow related to Messala as well, but those identifications are at best suspect. See Brown at 186, nn. 27–30, though Messala's renown for linguistic knowledge adds some credibility to the alleged link.

l.43 In Roman legend, Latinus was king of Latium. Virgil claimed he was the son of the god Faunus and the nymph Marica. Latinus has also been identified as Aeneas' father-in-law.

l.46 Canusium, modern Canosa in Puglia, was allegedly founded by Diomede. Its inhabitants spoke both Greek and Oscan, a local dialect looked down upon by most Romans. See Brown at 187, nn. 27–30.

l.49 Quirinus was a deity of the Sabine community before the founding of Rome. He was later identified with Romulus, so he is an apt choice for direction on this point.

ll.53–54 It is unclear whether the "Alpinus" attacked here, as the scholiasts claimed, is the Furius mentioned by Catullus. The scholiasts further claimed that Catullus' Furius was A. Furius Bibaculus, an acidic, impoverished neoteric poet. These identifications remain controversial. See Alexander Heidel, "Catullus and Furius Bibaculus," *Classical Review* 15, 4 (May 1901): 215–17; Rudd (1966) at 289–90.

Memnon was the mythical son of Tithonus and Eos who was the king of the Ethiopians and Egypt. He fought with Troy in the Trojan War, during which he killed Antilochus but was later killed by Achilles.

The proper translation and interpretation of this passage remains murky, but a good guess is that damming the Rhine's headwaters is another twist on the trope of water as speech and that the Alpinus attacked here either came from the Alps or wrote about them (or both).

l.56 Pompey chose Spurius Maecius Tarpa in 55 B.C. to select and stage plays in a new theater. See Brown at 188, nn. 38–39.

ll.58–61 Fundanius is unknown, although he reappears in Book II, Satire 8. There is no obvious extant work being referred to here, but the pair Davus and Chremes were stock characters who appeared in many plays, including Plautus' *Trinummus*, Menander's *The Girl of Andrius*, and Terence's *Andria*. See C. W. Amerasinghe, "The Part of the Slave in Terence's Drama," *Greece & Rome* 19, 56 (June 1950): 62–72.

l.61 Gaius Asinius Pollio (76 B.C.–4 A.D.) was a renowned historian, tragedian, orator, and poet—as well as a statesman supportive of Octavian. He served as consul in 40 B.C. and helped to bring about the treaty of Brundisium between Antony and Octavian. He was the first major supporter of Virgil and wrote a well-regarded but not extant history of Rome's civil wars. He also founded Rome's first public library.

l.68 Marcus Terentius Varro (116–27 B.C.) was a supporter of Pompey who later reconciled with Caesar. A wide-ranging intellectual and a prolific writer, very little of his work survives; we have only fragments of his influential *Menippean Satires*. Oddly, Horace is referring in this line to a much more obscure Varro, Publius Terentius Varro (82–37 B.C.), who we know wrote several long poems, but as far as we know did not write satire. Perhaps this reference is an inside joke, or perhaps we are missing key information.

l.77 Lucius Accius (170–?86 B.C.) was a prominent Roman tragedian. Very little of his work survives.

l.80 Quintus Ennius (239–169 B.C.) was a major Roman poet most known for his epic *Annales*, but he also wrote tragedies, comedies, and satires.

l.93 Cassius is unknown.

l.107. Romans would invert a stile (stylus) to erase errors on a tablet with the blunt end.

l.109 Arbuscula was an actress probably well past her prime at the time of this satire. See Brown at 192, nn.76–77.

ll.114–117 Demetrius, Pontilius, and Fannius are unknown. Given his careful criticism of his critics, it is safe to assume that Horace was using pseudonyms.

l.120 Plotius and Varius were poets discussed above at I. 5, l. 65.

l.121 C. Valgius Rufus wrote elegies and epigrams, and may have been quite young at the time of this satire since he served as consul in 12 B.C.. He was highly regarded by his contemporaries, but it appears he never wrote the great epic they expected from him.

l.122 Octavius Musa was a historian. See Brown at 193, nn. 82–83.

l.123 Aristius Fuscus is the comic poet who thwarts Horace's efforts to separate himself from "the bore" in Book I, Satire 9.

l.124 A Viscus Thurinus appears as a dinner guest in the final satire, but otherwise the Viscus brothers are lost to posterity.

ll.126–127 For Pollio see l. 61; for Messala see l. 41.

ll.128–129 Bibulus may be the stepson of Brutus. Servius is probably either the son of a famous jurist, Servius Sulpicius Rufus or an erotic poet mentioned by Ovid. Furnius may be a skilled orator mentioned by Plutarch. *See* Brown at 193, n. 86.

❧ BOOK II

Satire I

l.6 C. Trebatius Testa (?84 B.C.–4 A.D) was a renowned lawyer and a protégé of Cicero. Cicero dedicated *Topica* to Trebatius and recommended him as a legal advisor to Julius Caesar. Horace may be tweaking him at lines 9–12 based on a letter from Cicero to Trebatius. Cic.Fam.7.10.2 Dec *"Sed tu in re militari multo es cautior quam in advocationibus qui neque in Oceano notare volueris studiossimus homo natandi"* ("But you are more careful in military than legal matters, like a man who most eagerly wants to swim in the ocean but does not"). Muecke speculates, probably correctly, at 102 n.7 that the joke in these lines extends to the recommendation of unwatered wine since Cicero also refers to drinking with Trebatius.

l.6 The term "praescribe" (translated as "Decide") has a primary meaning of "inscribe," as in making an inscription on a legal document, but it has many other meanings, including one close to the English term "prescribe" (make a claim). Its precise meaning here is not clear. Fairclough renders it as "give me advice," Alexander as "tell me," Muecke as "give a ruling," and Rudd as "Please advise me." In context, the term almost certainly has legal overtones, so Muecke's version is probably the best of the four, but I think the compact and less tentative "Decide," as in "decide a case," better catches the spirit of the original.

l.17 Horace's reference to Trebatius as *pater optime* (literally "best father," here "Most wise advisor") is a reminder that Horace was still a young man at this time and that Trebatius was senior to Horace in all respects that mattered in Roman society.

l.18 "Vires" (here "motivation") is a supple word commonly translated as "force" or "power," and most translators have selected one of these two terms. While on a simplistic level this choice is unassailably "correct," it overlooks the fact that it doesn't make much sense in context to turn to a term that connotes physical power or force, particularly since in lines 20–23 Horace demonstrates that he is perfectly capable of writing exactly the kind of verse that Trebatius is urging him to write. Accordingly, it seems to me that here Horace is using a standard shorthand for the phrase *vires animi*, which is similar to our "will power" or "force of will." *Oxford Latin Dictionary*, 2076 at 22a. This interpretation escapes the necessity of viewing lines 18–23 as caustic, oddly ironic, or just plain stupid. Others will surely disagree with my assessment.

l.28 "Flaccus" is a reference to Horace, whose full name was "Quintus Horatius Flaccus." The term means "droopy," an adjective often used by Romans to describe donkeys. Perhaps here we have a self-deprecatory contrast with the trope of Octavian as a kicking stallion.

ll.33–34 Commentators debate whether Nomentanus is a reference to a Cassius Nomentanus who may have lived into Horace's time or to a Lucilian character. See Muecke at 105, n.22. The presence of a Nomentanus at the banquet in Book II, Satire 8 makes the Lucilian interpretation unlikely, although some stirring of a Lucilian echo is not out of the question. Moreover, for Horace the recently dead who were well known were much safer targets than the living given the potentially high legal and political penalties for offending people.

ll.37-40 Milonius does not refer to any known historical figure. It is plausible that he is a stock character whose name derives from "mel" (honey or sweetness) because dancing was considered disreputable and effeminate among Roman traditionalists. "Lamps divide" is a description of seeing double while drunk.

ll.40–42 In mythology Castor was the identical twin of Pollux. They were very different despite their genetic identity.

l.43 For background on Lucilius, see Coffey at 35–62.

ll.44–45 A foot is a unit of metrical poetry, hence "to fetter/words in feet" is a way of saying "writing metrical poetry." For a general description of Latin prosody, see Frederic William Westaway, *Quantity and Accent in the Pronunciation of Latin* (Ithaca, N.Y.: Cornell University Library Digital Collections, 2007).

l.50 Votive tablets usually showed threats that were miraculously overcome by courage or divine intervention. See Muecke at 107, nn.32–34.

ll.52–61 Scholars have disagreed about translation of this section. Muecke summarizes the scholarship and concludes that Horace is claiming "descent not from the farmer-colonists, but from one of their war-like neighbors." Muecke at 107, n.34. I disagree, and read the passage as Horace aligning himself with the settlers sent by Rome who were influenced by both preexisting tribes, thus making this section another example of Horace's penchant for balancing extremes.

ll.62–73 This section is the first clear example in Book II of Horace's use of self-deprecatory humor as a technique of satire. This technique becomes a common one in Book II and is much easier to use given the reliance of Book II on a dialogue format. Self-deprecatory humor not only offers the only truly safe target for a satirist, it is a highly effective technique when used well because it persuades the reader that the narrator/target is both self-aware and humble, thus credible.

l.75 The phrase "jurors' urns" refers to juror voting on a verdict by putting a tablet containing a judgment into an urn.

ll.73–79 Muecke notes ambiguity as to whether Albucius is a poisoner or a victim. See Muecke at 109, n.48. I have followed the view that "Albuci" is genitive, not objective, and therefore a poisoner, not a poisoner's victim, based on my view that structurally Cervius, Canidia, Albucius, and Turius appear to be elements of a list designed to prove the proposition that bad actors, when provoked, will use their special means of retaliation. Moreover, the Albucius of Book II, Satire 2, probably the same person, is clearly viewed by Horace as a nasty fellow. See II.2. l. 104. Fairclough and Alexander straddle the fence with the ambiguous "poison of Albucius," but it would seem odd for Horace to include an innocent with this nasty pack of scoundrels. There is no extratextual evidence either way. Cervius is unknown, and Canidia is the witch featured at the end of Book I, Satire 8.

l.78 Turius was a notoriously severe judge tentatively identified by Muecke as the judge for a major scandal case in 75 B.C.—perhaps another illustration of a pattern of satirizing those safely dead but recent enough to be remembered. See Muecke at 109, n.49.

l.86 Muecke identifies Scaeva as a common Roman *cognomen*. Rudd notes a pun on righthandedness and lefthandedness that I have been unable to replicate. See Muecke at 109, n.53; Rudd at 293, n.16.

ll.107–109 The phrase "he who earned his name by crushing Carthage" is a periphrasis for Publius Cornelius Scipio Africanus Major, commonly referred to as Scipio or Scipio Africanus, a general who led the destruction of Carthage in the Second Punic War.

ll.110–111 Q. Caecilius Metellus Macedonius and L. Cornelius Lentulus Lupus were prominent politicians and opponents of Scipio.

l.118 Gaius Laelius was a general and ally of Scipio who was favorably depicted in several of Cicero's works.

Satire 2

l.4 The name Ofellus has been attributed to a historical figure of Oscan origin, although that identification is uncertain. If the name is fictional, it may be a play on "ofella" (pork cutlet). See Muecke at 116–17, n.2.

l.5 The phrase "crassaque Minerva" (here "rustic wisdom") is a reference to Minerva, the goddess, and hence the source, of wisdom. The deflating adjective *crassaque* (from which we get our "crass") means "thickened," "fat" or, less frequently, "opaque." Any attempt at "literal translation" will miss the many nuances of this phrase. I settled on "rustic wisdom" because "rustic" tends to have the type of negative undertones that Horace intends. One could argue that a more derisive term is in order here.

l.12 This satire is an anomaly in Book II in that it is not a dialogue and seems closer in spirit to the three "diatribe" satires that open Book I. Since there is no punctuation in the original text, it is difficult to tell whether "cur hoc" (here "Why do that?") that I have attributed to an anonymous member of the audience reflects Horace's intention or whether it was intended as a rhetorical question. I chose to view it as an interjection for three reasons. First, it comes closely on the heels of "boni" (here "dear associates"), a direct address to an audience, and a reply shortly thereafter seems natural, although not essential. Second, my interpretation injects a little more humor into this line, since it is unclear whether the anonymous foil is questioning the search for truth or the search for truth *on an empty stomach*. Third, the term "disquirite" (here "seek the truth") has some flavor of Greek philosophical dialogues, so a reply in the next line also seems natural. Since it struck me as a coin flip on the merits, I went for the funnier version and felt that Horace would have blessed the rationale, if not the choice.

The opening line is ironic. As tangled as the following lines are in my version, the original is worse. For instance, one sentence is missing a verb. One could also argue that the "evidence" for the proposition stated in lines 13–14 is something of a non sequitur.

ll.25–27 This is a reference to "mulsum," a mixture of the finest wine and honey. See Muecke at 118, n.15.

l.36 Commentators agree that "lagois" refers to some sort of exotic bird, but they don't have a clue as to which one. Muecke uses the improbable "ptarmigan," Fairclough and Rudd use "foreign grouse," and Alexander uses the "migrating grouse." I have followed the convention of using "foreign" so that the bird's exotic nature is flagged, but thought that birds smaller than grouse—shunned by hungry Americans but still prized by Italians—were more probable. See generally Emily Gowers, *The Loaded Table: Representations of Food in Roman Literature* (Oxford: Clarendon Press, 1993).

ll.47–50 Bass caught between the two bridges of the Tiber were highly prized for no reason other than social expectations. See Muecke at 120, n.32.

l.64 Harpies were voracious birds with the faces of women.

l.66 Siroccos, or Austral winds, were the warm southern winds of summer and autumn originating in northern Africa. Perhaps contrary to modern associations, they were associated with disease and death.

ll.67–68 Uncastrated pigs take on an undesirable scent today known as "boar taint," which is caused by accumulation of androstenone and skatole in the flesh. See "These Little Pigs Get Special Care from Norwegians," *Wall Street Journal*, August 6, 2007, at 1.

l.79 A praetor was a magistrate subordinate to the consuls. The referent here is unclear; it could be an inside joke or it could be a shorthand way of saying "big shots."

l.88 Commentators debate whether Avidienus was a reference to a real person. Given that the name appears to be a play on the word "avidus" ("grasping"), it seems plausible that he is a fictional or composite character. See Muecke at 123, n.55.

l.91 A cornel is the acidic but edible berry of a tree from the dogwood genus.

l.102 The source of this proverbial saying is unknown.

l.106 Probably, but not necessarily, the Albucius of II.1, l. 78.

l.109 This Naevius is unknown and probably different from the Naevius of I.1. l. 136.

l.119 The phrase *cena dubia* (here "dinners served with doubt") was a standard phrase translated by Fairclough as "puzzle feast," by Muecke as "a perplexing dinner," by Alexander as "a meal in which there's too much to choose," and by Rudd as "problem meal." Obviously, there is no easy English phrase to describe a meal of many overwhelming exotic choices, so I used quotation marks to flag it as a term of art and linked the two root words of "dinner" and "doubt" as best as I could.

ll.153–154 Describing someone desperate as too poor to buy a noose was a standard joke of this era.

l.156 Trausius is unknown.

l.158 Somewhere in the vicinity of this line, the tone begins to change in an interesting way. Horace's guise of merely reporting Ofellus' standard lecture starts to slip once he starts in on Roman excess and he seem to start identifying with the man he was ridiculing. Lines 171–174 become more personal and feel like a fair description of Horace's lifestyle as discussed elsewhere in the *Satires*. Lines 174–179 remove any real doubt about his identification with Ofellus when he claims Ofellus is going through what was the most searing experience in Horace's life—the confiscation of his family's land. In lines 184–186 he favorably portrays laziness, a charge that Horace has made against him many times before, perhaps most forcefully in Damasippus' opening indictment of Horace's work habits in Book II, Satire 3.

l.193 Ceres was the goddess of grain. The *lanx satura*, a tightly packed food from which satura ("satire") is probably derived, was offered to Ceres to express gratitude for a good harvest. See Freudenberg at 45.

l.209 Umbrenus is unknown.

Satire 3

l.1 In these opening lines Horace takes an interesting step by making himself the subject of his own satire. Except for a few comments in Book I, this technique is new. It has many advantages for Horace—his target can't sue or provoke political retribution, and it opens up a productive vein of humor. As many comedians and politicians have discovered, self-deprecatory humor is inherently appealing to most audiences—it tends to reflect self-awareness, humility, and lack of ulterior motive. It is worth noting that Horace's embrace of the dialogue format in Book II creates an opportunity for other characters to comment upon the poet's foibles and shortcomings, and hence opens up multiple opportunities for self-deprecatory humor. Since philosophers tended to follow the format of Socratic dialogues, it also provides Horace with a tool for lampooning the pretensions of all schools of philosophy from Stoicism to Epicureanism—and pretty much everything in between.

Commentators often miss the humor of these lines. For instance, Muecke believes "the reproach of unproductivity rings true because elsewhere Horace has made a virtue of writing little," at 132, n.1, when in fact the number of Horace's masterpieces speaks for itself. In any fair reading, Horace portrays Damasippus as a buffoon for confusing quality with quantity.

l.3 From known texts, the verb "retexo" (here "unweaving") is found only in this line. Muecke argues that it refers to Penelope's web, which was not intended to be completed. See Muecke at 132, n.2.

l.7 Saturnalia was a popular Roman holiday originally celebrated on December 17 and eventually extended to a full week despite intermittent efforts by authorities to limit it. Among other ceremonies, it involved the untying of ropes that bound statues of Saturn—as well as the untying of many social constraints. Slaves were allowed special liberties during this time, cf. II.7, and it was a time of gift-giving and revelry, something like a combination of Mardi Gras and Christmas.

ll.17–19 Most commentators, including Rudd, Freudenberg and Muecke, seem quite sure that the reference in line 17 is to Plato the famed philosopher rather than Plato the comic playwright (428–327 B.C.) who was a rival of Aristophanes. This interpretation is almost surely wrong. Aside from falling into the trap of relying on history's judgments of relative importance in the face of incomplete information (little survives of Plato the comedian's work), this view overlooks

Horace's reverence for the poets of Old Comedy (as expressed in the opening of Book I, Satire 4) and his clear disdain for the philosophers, a point made extremely clearly in this satire and elsewhere in the *Satires*. The clincher for me is "invidiam" (here "envy") in line 20 of the question that follows this list. Why would Horace include Plato the philosopher in a list of three comic poets when it is far more logical that he would be adding a fourth renowned comic poet, and why would Damasippus be accusing him of *envy* of everyone on that list if Horace has no interest in joining the ranks of great philosophers?

ll.25–28 It is unclear whether this is a blessing or a curse, an ambiguity which is probably intentional. The reference to a barber is a joke that Damasippus will need a barber for his beard now that he has become a philosopher.

l.27 Damasippus was probably the speculator who appears in letters of Cicero. See Muecke 134 at n.16.

ll.29–30 The Arch of Janus in question—not to be confused with the still-standing Arch of Janus built in the early fourth century—was probably in the Forum and served as a location for a forerunner of modern stock and commodities exchanges.

l.35 Sisyphus, best known today for his punishment by unending labor in Hades, was a founder and king of Corinth who was notorious for treachery.

l.38 The amount of this bid was probably 100,000 sesterces. It is hard to create a modern equivalent, but as a frame of reference in the reign of Augustus a knight needed to have 400,000 sesterces of property and a senator needed to have 1,000,000 sesterces of property.

l.42 Mercury was the god of commerce. The term *merx* means "goods" or "wares," hence the name of the god as well as "mercantile" and "merchandise."

l.54 It is not clear whether Stertinius was real or fictional. It is perhaps instructive that "stertere" is the Latin word for "snore."

l.60 The Fabrician bridge extended from the Campus Martius to the Tiber island. It was built in 62 B.C. and still stands. It is also referred to today as "the Jewish bridge."

l.62 Romans considered the right hand good and the left hand evil. Our "sinister" comes directly from the Latin *sinister* for "left."

l.71 Chrysippus of Soli (?280–?207 B.C.) was a student of Zeno of Citium and a founder of Stoicism. Of his over 700 reported works, none survive in their entirety. For a brief but solid overview of Stoicism, see "Stoicism," in Paul Edwards, ed., *The Encyclopedia of Philosophy* (New York: Macmillan, 1967), 8: 19–22.

l.71 The Stoics took their name from the Painted Portico (or "Stoa") in the Agora at Athens where Zeno of Citium taught. See Muecke at 139, n.44.

ll.95–99 This passage refers to a famous incident during a performance of Pacuvius' *Iliona* in which a ghost appears to ask his mother for burial. The actor playing Iliona was dead drunk, and the audience shouted out the familiar lines to fill the void. Fufius and Catienus were actors performing in a revival of the play.

l.111 Nerius may be a reference to a man known to be a quaestor in 49 B.C.

l.112 Cicuta is undoubtedly a stock character; the word means "hemlock" in Latin.

l.114 Proteus is the shape-shifting god of the sea.

l.122 From context we know Perellius is a moneylender, but we don't know whether he is real or fictional. A Perellius Fausta accused Virgil of plagiarism of Ennius, but there is no evidence to link this reference to that Perellius.

l.133 Hellebore (also known today as "Christmas rose" or "Lenten rose" although not a member of the rose genus) is a flowering plant that grows in most of southern Europe. It has been used as a poison and a medicine, and some speculate that it killed Alexander the Great. Its appropriateness as a remedy for the "madness" described in the preceding lines would be clear to an educated Roman because he would know that in Greek mythology Melampus of Rylos used hellebore to save the daughters of the king of Argos from Dionysian madness.

l.134 There were three towns called Anticyra in Greece. The largest, famous for hellebore, was in the district of Phocis on the Gulf of Corinth.

l.136 This line may refer to Staberius Eros (83–34 B.C.), who was a freedman and a grammarian.

l.140 Arrius was a rich contemporary of Cicero who hosted a banquet for several thousand people. See Muecke at 142, n.85.

l.141 For information on Rome's importation of corn, see Geoffrey Rickman, *The Corn Supply of Ancient Rome* (Oxford: Clarendon Press, 1980).

l.161 Aristippus (?435–?366 B.C.) was a Greek philosopher and associate of Socrates born in Cyrene, which is now eastern Libya. He (or possibly his grandson by the same name) was the founder of the Cyrenaic school, which endorsed hedonism and egoism. This school differed from the Epicureans in that they denied that we should defer short-term pleasure for the sake of long-term pleasure. None of his writings are extant.

ll.161–164 This anecdote illustrates the Cyrenaics' preference for short-term pleasure discussed above at l. 161.

l.186 Chian and Falernian were fine wines.

ll.211–224 In Greek mythology Orestes was the son of Agamemnon and Clytemnestra. Although his story varies from teller to teller, in Homer's version Orestes discovered eight years after the Trojan War that Clytemnestra had murdered Agamemnon with an axe; Orestes then killed Clytemnestra. In Aeschylus' version, Orestes returned with his friend Pylades after two decades to seek revenge.

The Furies, three goddesses of vengeance, were Tisiphone, Megaera, and Alecto. They were terrifying figures with heads wreathed in serpents, but fair in their judgments. When Orestes prayed to Apollo, Athena intervened and transformed the Furies into the Eumenides, protectors of the suppliant.

ll.225–230 Horace is probably being mischievous with the recently dead again by making Opimius a pauper. The Opimius family spawned a long line of brutal but increasingly less successful public figures. Since their run had pretty much petered out by the time of Horace, they were a fairly safe target for tweaking. The consulship in 121 B.C, of one member of the family, Lucius Opimius, coincided with a legendary vintage of wine that became known as the "vinum Opimianum."

l.248 Rice was a somewhat exotic import used primarily as a medicine. See Muecke at 148, n.155.

l.255 The Craterus referred to here was a distinguished Greek physician not to be confused with the more famous general of Alexander the Great.

l.261 The Lares, also known as *genii loci*, were Roman deities protecting the house and family who were generally thought to be sons of Hermes and Lara. Most Romans had small statues of the Lares in their homes and generally put them on their tables for meals. Over time the jurisdiction of the Lares extended more broadly outside the home and their images and roles became confused with other deities.

l.268 Servius Oppidius is unknown.

l.282 The Penates were originally gods of the storeroom, but eventually expanded their jurisdiction to the entire household and assumed a role similar to the Lares after the Lares indulged in greater territorial ambitions. See l. 261 above.

l.291 The cheapness of Servius Oppidius is being mocked here because lupines, vetch, and beans were inexpensive foods. Grain lupines (sometimes spelled "lupins"), also known as "lupine beans," have been cultivated for thousands of years in Europe, Africa, and the Middle East. Lupin seeds were found in a pharaoh's tomb in a 6,000-year-old pyramid. Many varieties of the genus, however, are poisonous. Vetch is another grain legume resembling red lentils, although it is much more bitter and tend to be foods only for the desperately hungry.

ll.297–298 This story seems to be a reference to a popular fable, but no source has been identified.

l.299 Agrippa was one of the most powerful and respected figures of Horace's time, and this reference lacks any irony or satirical intent—undoubtedly a prudent choice. Marcus Vipsanius Agrippa (63–12 B.C.), a Roman statesman and general, was a childhood friend and close associate of Octavian. He refused a triumph offered to him for his military exploits, but accepted his first consulship in 37 B.C. In 33 B.C he was elected aedile, and engaged in a series of highly popular public works projects around Rome. Agrippa was also instrumental in Octavian's victory at Actium in 31 B.C. His political fortunes subsequently slipped in the intrigues of Rome, but at the time Horace was writing this satire, Agrippa was at the height of his power and fame.

l.300 The dialogue interjected here is one of the most famous in classical literature for illustrating Horace's general point about much apparent reason being madness.

ll.311–319 Achilles, the greatest hero of Homer's *Iliad*, was the son of mortal Peleus and the Nereid Thetis. Priam was the King of Troy during the Trojan War. Menelaus was the King of Sparta during the Trojan War. Ajax was the King of Salamis and second only to Achilles among Agamemnon's warriors. The Achaeans were the people ruled by Agamemnon. They were from the northern part of the Peloponnese.

l.329 Teucer was the nephew of Priam and fought with his half-brother Ajax in the Trojan War.

l.365 Bellona was an early Italian war goddess worshipped with wild dances and orgiastic rites involving self-mutilation. When her temple was destroyed in 48 B.C remains of human flesh were found. See Muecke at 156, n.222.

l.374 The Vicus Tuscus (here "Tuscan Alley") was an alley that went from the Forum to the Velabrum. Based on Horace's comment here and a blunter comment by Plautus (Plaut. Curc. 482: "*in Tusco vico ibi sunt homines qui ipsi sese venditant*"), it apparently was the haunt of male prostitutes.

l.376 The Velabrum is a former swamp between the northwest slope of the Palatine and Capitoline hills. It was short on shrines and long on commercial establishments, particularly for the sale of food and wine.

ll.393–397 M. Clodius Aesopus's son inherited 20,000,000 sesterces from his father, who was a renowned tragic actor. See Muecke at 158, n. 239. If there had been tabloids in ancient Rome, Metella (Caecilia Metella Celer) would have been one of their stars. She was the daughter of Quintus Caecilius Metellus Celer and his notorious wife Clodia. Shortly after her wedding, Metella started an affair with one of her conservative husband's political opponents. They divorced amid public scandal in 45 B.C. Metella later seduced associates of Julius Caesar for political purposes, took a poet named Ticida as a lover who called her Perilla when he wrote about her, and eventually ended up sleeping with Aesopus' son in exchange for financial support of her family.

l.400 See l.140 above. Nothing is known of his sons.

l.416 Polemon was a second-century B.C Athenian Stoic philosopher. In his profligate youth he burst in on a lecture by Xenocrates with the intention of disrupting it, but became enthralled and eventually succeeded Xenocrates as the leader of his school.

ll.449–451 These lines describe a game in which people squeezed apple seeds between their fingers to see how high they would go, with the seed going the highest being the best omen for love. See Muecke at 161, n. 273.

ll.458–459 Nothing is known of this tale.

ll.464–474 This is a cryptic passage. Menenius, an ally of Coriolanus, was consul in 503 B.C and his son was consul in 439 B.C. Among his other achievements, he was known for bridging disagreements with the lower classes. Since this sentence is referring to the opinion of a Stoic on self-centered people, it is fair to assume that he is writing them off as another type of crazy person, but we seem to lack the information necessary for understanding the reference to Menenius' clan.

l.477 Quartan fevers were relatively mild and recurred every third day. See Muecke at 163, n. 290.

l.487 Damasippus is placing Stertinius just beneath the Seven Sages. Although the ancients hotly debated exactly who was deserving of this lofty title, the consensus was Solon of Athens, Chilon of Sparta, Thales of Miletus, Bias of Priene, Cleobulus of Lindos, Pittaeus of Mitylene, and Periander of Corinth.

ll.498–501 This story from mythology is best known from Euripides' *The Bacchae* and Ovid's *Metamorphoses*.

l.509 Turbo was probably a short gladiator. See Muecke at 165, n. 310.

Satire 4

l.1 For debate about the identity of Catius, see Muecke at 167–68.

l.4 Pythagoras, in addition to being an influential mathematician, founded a mystical/philosophical group. Since none of his writings survive, the exact tenets of his teachings are unknown, but generally secondary evidence supports the view that his followers believed in the application of mathematics to all phenomena and, perhaps more relevant here, refused to eat meat or beans.

l.5 This oblique reference is to Socrates. Muecke notes that the extended phrase is necessary because the name "Socrates" could not fit into Horace's hexameter, a consideration that has my utmost sympathy. See Muecke at 168, nn.2-3. Anytus was not even one of Socrates' principal accusers.

ll.28, 35 Falernian was a fine wine.

l.34 Aufidius is unknown.

l.42 Coan was another fine wine.

ll.45–48 Baiae, Circeii, and Misenum were towns on the Campanian coast. The Lucrine lake was close to Baiae. Tarentum is at the site of modern Taranto in southern Italy.

l.49 This is a frequently mistranslated passage. The word "patulis" (here "gaping") is almost surely intended to refer to opened shells exposing the scallop meat.

l.57 Umbria is a region of central Italy.

l.58 The Laurentian marsh is near Rome.

l.70 Massic was a variety of Falernian.

l.75 Sorrentine is another high quality wine.

l.94 Corycus is in southern Turkey.

l.96 Venafrum (modern Venafro) was a town in Campenia famous for supplying the best olive oil.

l.97 Tibur (modern Tivoli) was a town in Lazio near the falls of the river Aniene.

l.99 Picenum (modern Marche) was a region along the Adriatic between Ancona and the river Sangro.

l.101 Rudd notes that these grapes were not a local variety. They are mentioned by Columella and Pliny. See Rudd at 255, n.71.

l.102 The Alban Hills are about 20 km southeast of Rome.

l.121 Coveted purple dye from Tyre in Phoenicia.

ll.137–138 Water from fountains or springs as a trope for wisdom was often used in other Roman verse, such as the *Prologue* to Persius' *Satires*.

Satire 5

l.1 I can't bring myself to summarize all of Homer, but it is important to know that Ulysses is the returning hero, Penelope is his famously faithfully wife, and Tiresias is a seer. This satire is perhaps the first great spoof of Roman literature, although there was a long tradition of parodying Homer in Greek literature. See Coffey at 86.

ll.20–23 The Lares were the household gods.

l.27 "Dama" was a stock name for a slave.

ll.34–39 For an overview of Roman will-hunting, see Rudd at 225–27.

l.49 Quintus was Horace's *praenomen* (first name).

ll.59–62 Modern scholars tend to doubt early attribution of these quotations to the neoteric poet Furius Bibaculus. See Muecke at 185, n. 41.

l.74 Orcus was the god of the dead.

ll.85–86 Nasica and Coranus are unknown.

l.96 The Parthian Empire was the most formidable threat to Rome during Horace's era. At its height, Parthia included most of modern-day Iran and Iraq, as well as other parts of the Middle East. Strabo believed that the empire originated in modern-day Kurdistan, but in fact we know very little about Parthia's language, history, and culture. In 53 B.C. Rome failed in an attempt to invade Parthia, and the empires then battled intermittently for three centuries. During Rome's civil wars in the following years, a general who had opposed Caesar, Quintus Labienus, defected to Parthia and took several towns that had been conquered by Rome. Antony retaliated in 39 B.C. and Labienus was killed, but subsequent Roman advances suffered large casualties. In 20 B.C. Octavian finally entered into a peace treaty with Parthia. Most scholars believe Parthia was an irritant and an obstacle to eastern expansion of the Roman Empire, but not a true threat.

ll.131–132 The joke here is that Tiresias, who can see the future, is telling a story about events that have not yet occurred.

l.143 "Davus" is another stock name for a slave, and it is the name Horace chooses for his own fictional slave in Book II, Satire 7. The reference to "the comedy" is impossible to pin down since the name was used so often.

l.169 Proserpine was the goddess of the underworld.

Satire 6

ll.1–4 Readers should read these lines remembering that Horace lost his father's hard-earned land due to joining the losing side at the Battle of Philippi.

l.7 The son of Maia is Mercury. Some commentators miss that Horace is starting to put his tongue into his cheek here and that this reference is the set-up for the abrupt change in tone from the lofty invocation to the mockery beginning at line 12. Mercury is the god of commerce, and presumably received many grubby prayers along the lines of the ones at lines 12–20.

l.23 In this line "fatten" also has the sense of dulling and becoming self-satisfied.

l.34 Libitina was the goddess of death, corpses, and funerals.

l.36 Ianus was the god of doors, gates, beginnings, and endings.

l.49 It is not clear whether this parenthetical is tied to the preceding or following sentence.

l.54 The Esquiline was a former burial ground converted into a park and residential area where Maecenas had a grand home. It is the site of Book I, Satire 8.

l.58 Here "the second hour" means the second hour after dawn, a very early start for a late sleeper like Horace.

ll.63–64 Horace's patron Maecenas was actually running the daily operations of the Empire at the time this satire was probably written because Octavian had not yet returned from the Battle of Actium. See Muecke at 201, nn.38–39.

l.71 I stretched a little here to make the joke fit a contemporary tic. Literally, "hora quota est" is closer to "What hour is it?" I like to think Horace would forgive me, but this liberty may be a neurological effect of excessive composition of heroic couplets.

ll.72–73 These are the kinds of names given to gladiators.

l.81 *Rostra* was a platform for public addresses.

l.85 The Dacians were a people thriving in the area roughly approximating modern Romania. They consolidated their tribal leadership into a central government in order to resist the Romans, and largely fended Rome off until they were finally conquered in 106 A.D. Around the time period of the composition of the *Satires* they had developed alliances with Antony against Octavian.

l.112 Lepos may have been one of Octavian's favorite dancers, but the evidence for that is shaky. The root of his name suggests charm or grace, a typical practice of actors in mimes, which were low comedies, not the silent sketches of today's mimes. See Muecke at 206, n.72.

ll.115–118 Horace is mimicking the kinds of subjects discussed in Greek philosophical dialogues, particularly those of Plato.

l.120 Cervius is unknown.

ll.125–180 These lines track Aesop's fable of the country mouse and the city mouse fairly closely, although Horace embellishes many of the details to make the tale (no pun intended) more Roman, particularly in lines 160–168.

Satire 7

ll.1–4 The exact context of these opening lines is unclear, although not critical to understanding the satire. "Davus" is a stock name in Roman drama for a slave. It's not clear whether Davus' opening remark is a reference to an ongoing conversation or to Davus listening over a long period of time. Given how much pent-up sentiment Davus expresses in this satire, the latter interpretation is probably more likely. Also, it is not clear whether Horace's first response is genuine or playful. It could be that Horace can't recognize Davus because it is Saturnalia, a time of costumes and changed roles. It could be that Davus is approaching Horace in the dark or at a distance. It could be, though, that Horace is seriously or playfully expressing surprise at Davus' proposal.

l.5 The nuances of this line are not entirely clear, but it may be a play upon some proverb or catchphrase.

l.6 "December's freedom" is a reference to the Roman holiday of Saturnalia.

l.8 Priscus is unknown and may be fictional. His name was a common *cognomen*, though it may be a play on the Latin word "priscus" meaning "ancient" or "old-fashioned."

ll.8–26 Davus is mimicking some of Horace' favorite rhetorical techniques. See Muecke at 215, nn.6–20.

l.20 Vertumnus, the god of seasons, change, and plant growth, could change his shape at will. In Ovid's *Metamorphoses* he uses this ability to seduce Pomona.

l.21 Volanerius is unknown.

ll.29–36 Davus is now not just imitating Horace's style, but throwing Horace's own words back at him by echoing Horace's critique of others that opened Book I, Satire 1. See I.1, ll. 1–30.

l.50 Mulvius is unknown. The elite segment of Roman society was filled with hangers-on.

ll.54–56 This image is supposed to reduce him to the level of an animal, probably a pig or dog.

l.63 500 drachmas was not a lot of money for a slave.

l.67 The joke here is that Davus does not have direct access to the philosopher he is quoting—it is second-hand from the philosopher's slave and therefore unreliable for multiple reasons.

The scholiasts believed that Crispinus was a reference to an inept poet and philosopher named Aretalogus. In the extant literature there is also one reference to a Greek rhetorician by the name of Crispinus. Freudenberg argues that the name is an anagram for Chrysippus, the Stoic philosopher. See Freudenberg at 40.

ll.70–71 The phrase "nailed upon a cross" is not metaphorical; it was a standard method of Roman execution generally reserved for slaves.

l.84 Like "Davus," "Dama" was a stock name for a slave in Roman drama.

ll.124–128 Even within the category of "slave," Roman society had some hierarchy. See Freudenberg at 51.

l.157 These names are typical of gladiators.

l.192 Sabine Farm was the farm that Maecenas gave to Horace.

Satire 8

l.2 Nasidienus Rufus may be fictional, although there is a first-century inscription with this name. If it is fictional, it may be a play on *nasus* ("nose") and *rufus* ("red") that suggests familiarity with his supply of fine wine.

There have also been some who think that this name may be a reference to Salvidienus Rufus, a man of equestrian rank who rose to great power and fame under Octavian. When Antony reconciled with Octavian, he disclosed that Rufus had offered to betray Octavian and side with Antony. Octavian then recalled Rufus on a pretext in 40 B.C. and let Rufus commit suicide after being condemned to death. Approximately ten years later, when this satire was being written, Rufus was safely dead and permanently out of favor with Octavian, so he was a very safe target for satire if he inspired this character.

l.8 Boar was a luxury. Lucania was a region of southern Italy between the Tyrrhenian Sea and the Gulf of Taranto.

l.10 Austral winds are southern winds. The adjective "leni" (here "gentle") is necessary to distinguish this wind from the more ominous siroccos mentioned many other times in the *Satires*.

l.12 Coan was a fine wine and wine lees were dregs used as a condiment.

l.17 Muecke notes that maple was considered a fine, but probably not the very best, wood by Romans of this era. See Muecke at 230–231, n. 11. Muecke believes that it is "unlikely that we are meant to think badly of Nasidienus for having a maple table," above at 231, which would undoubtedly be true in an ordinary narrative. In the context of this satire, however, in which the host is trying to roll out only the very best of everything, a maple table is probably either a subtle sign that there has been a small lapse in taste or that the host's social climbing is not yet complete.

l.21 Muecke describes Caecuban as the "best Roman wine, from a single vineyard in southern Latium." See Muecke at 231, n. 15.

l.22 Slaveboys were often the subject of considerable sexual attention by their masters and guests. "Hydaspes" is a river in India; a slaveboy from that part of the world would be highly exotic and therefore more sexually desirable in the eyes of many Romans.

ll.23–26 Attic maidens were involved in rituals for Ceres, the goddess of grain and alcohol. Chian was a fine wine. "Alcon" was a stock slave name similar to "Davus."

l.27 Alban and Falernian were fine wines.

l.30 Fundanius is unknown.

ll.33–37 There is confusion about which Viscus this is and we have no clue about Servilius Balatro and Vibidius. The Latin word "balatro" means "jester" and hence there is reason to believe that Balatro is a stock character. The amusing derivation of Porcius should be clear. Commentators cannot agree even whether the Nomentanus here is the same as the Nomentanus mentioned elsewhere in the *Satires*. See generally Muecke at 232–33, nn.21–23. Varius was a poet highly regarded by Horace and others. Although his work has not survived, he made an important contribution to Western literature by ignoring Virgil's instruction that his unfinished *Aeneid* be destroyed.

l.47 The meaning of "ilia" here is unclear. Given the persistence of its meaning in medical terminology I have opted for "organs" over roe, flanks and other alternatives used by other translators. Organs also strike me as more exotic and off-putting, and hence more appropriate here, but that reflects my personal tastes.

l.55 "Parochus" (here "keeper of the food") was the Latin word for someone hired to provide provisions, as in Book I, Satire 5. Its use here to describe the host should probably be viewed as a dig, a sign that the function reflects some sense of obligation rather than true generosity. Rudd correctly points out that the host's reaction to this demand is negative not due to stinginess, as many have assumed, but to fear that excessive wine is damaging their palates too much for them to appreciate his gourmet offerings. See Rudd at 219.

l.62 Cups from Allifae were common and probably large. See Muecke at 234–35, n.39.

l.73 "Garum" was made with fish offal left in a jar in the ground to ferment, and was very popular. Scandinavians and Vietnamese use somewhat similar recipes that tend to repel those who did not grow up eating such a sauce.

l.78 Methymnean was another high-quality product.

l.79 Rocket is a pungent herb and elecampane a bitter root.

l.81 Curtillus is unknown.

ll.98–99 Here the image of the uplifted nose suggests primal greed. The name "Nasidienus" may have a hint of this image as well.

l.115 Asking for slippers was a sign that he was going to leave the table, but not the room. See Muecke at 237, n.77.

l.140 Canidia was a witch, a poisoner, and the star of the end of Book I, Satire 8.

Sources

Editions of Horace are listed by the name of the editor.

Alexander, Sidney. *The Complete Odes and Satires of Horace.* Princeton, N.J.: Princeton University Press, 1996.

Brown, P. Michael. *Horace Satires I.* Warminster: Aris & Phillips, 1993.

Coffey, Michael, *Roman Satire.* Bristol: Bristol Classical Press, 1976.

Fairclough, H. R. *Horace, Satires, Epistles, and Ars Poetica.* Cambridge, Mass.: Harvard University Press, 1929.

Freudenberg, Kirk. *Satires of Rome.* Cambridge: Cambridge University Press, 2001.

Muecke, Frances. *Horace Satires II.* Warminster: Aris & Phillips, 1993.

Rudd, Niall. *The Satires of Horace.* Cambridge: Cambridge University Press, 1966.

Rudd, Niall. *Horace: Satires and Epistles.* New York: Penguin, 1973.

Schlegel, Catherine. *Satire and the Threat of Speech.* Madison: University of Wisconsin Press, 2005.

Acknowledgments

I am incredibly grateful to the large number of people who helped me with this project. Richard Thomas, Charles Martin, A. E. Stallings, and Anthony Lombardy provided assistance concerning the meaning of the original text. Deborah Warren and Laura Mali-Astrue assisted me with both the original text and other aspects of this translation. X. J. Kennedy and Len Krisak offered substantial suggestions for revisions of the first third of the manuscript. My online and in-person workshops (Eratosphere, Gazebo, and the Powow River Poets) provided considerable input, and many members of these groups provided advice outside the workshops, including Annie Bien, Mildred Nash, David Berman, Stephen Scaer, Duncan MacLaurin, Gregory Dowling, and Ed Conti. Catherine Tufariello, Rachel Hadas, Brad Leithauser and R. S. Gwynn also provided advice on parts of the manuscript. Paul Lepisto graciously answered questions about olive oil. Melissa Balmain carefully proofread the entire manuscript and saved me from an astounding number of small humiliations. Several anonymous reviewers provided important suggestions. Finally, Wyatt Prunty, Michael Peich, and Rhina Espaillat provided inspiration in moments of doubt.

Sections from this manuscript have appeared or will soon appear in *First Things*, *Literary Imagination*, *Measure*, *The New Criterion*, *Evansville Review*, and *Alimentum*. Aralia Press has published the opening of Book II, Satire 3 as "Damasippus Reprimands Horace" in a limited edition.